CW01103017

PULSE: An Ada-based Distributed Operating System

Academic Press Rapid Manuscript Reproduction

This is volume 26 in A.P.I.C. Studies in Data Processing
General Editors: Fraser Duncan *and* M. J. R. Shave
A complete list of titles in this series appears at the end of this volume

PULSE: An Ada-based Distributed Operating System

D. Keeffe G. M. Tomlinson
I. C. Wand A. J. Wellings

Department of Computer Science
University of York
York, England

1985

ACADEMIC PRESS
(Harcourt Brace Jovanovich, Publishers)
London Orlando San Diego New York
Toronto Montreal Sydney Tokyo

COPYRIGHT © 1985, BY ACADEMIC PRESS INC. (LONDON) LTD.
ALL RIGHTS RESERVED.
NO PART OF THIS PUBLICATION MAY BE REPRODUCED OR
TRANSMITTED IN ANY FORM OR BY ANY MEANS, ELECTRONIC
OR MECHANICAL, INCLUDING PHOTOCOPY, RECORDING, OR
ANY INFORMATION STORAGE AND RETRIEVAL SYSTEM, WITHOUT
PERMISSION IN WRITING FROM THE PUBLISHER.

ACADEMIC PRESS INC. (LONDON) LTD.
24-28 Oval Road
LONDON NW1 7DX

United States Edition published by
ACADEMIC PRESS, INC.
Orlando, Florida 32887

BRITISH LIBRARY CATALOGUING IN PUBLICATION DATA
PULSE : an ada-based distributed operating system.— —
   (APIC studies in data processing; 26)
   1. Electronic data processing—Distributed
processing   2. Microcomputers   3. Operating
systems (Computers)
I. Keeffe, D.   II. Series
001.64'25   QA76.9.D5
ISBN 0-12-402970-1

LIBRARY OF CONGRESS CATALOGING-IN-PUBLICATION DATA
Main entry under title:
PULSE: an Ada-based distributed operating system.
   (APIC studies in data processing ; no. 26)
   Bibliography: p.
   Includes index.
   1. PULSE (Computer operating system)   2. Ada
(computer program language)   3. Electronic data
processing—Distributed processing.   I. Keeffe, D.
II. Title: PULSE.   III. Series: A.P.I.C. studies
in data processing ; no. 26)
QA76.76.O63P85   1985   005.4'46   85-47930
ISBN 0-12-402970-1 (alk. paper)
PRINTED IN THE UNITED STATES OF AMERICA

85 86 87 88   9 8 7 6 5 4 3 2 1

Contents

Preface	xi
Acknowledgements	xiii

1. Introduction   1
  1.1 Distributed Computing   2
    1.1.1 Distributed System Definition   3
  1.2 The UNIX Operating System   4
    1.2.1 The File System   4
    1.2.2 The UNIX Process Model   6
  1.3 The Ada Programming Language   6
  1.4 The PULSE Distributed Operating System   8
    1.4.1 Methods of Distribution   9
    1.4.2 Ada and Distributed Systems   10
  1.5 Distributed Operating Systems   11
  1.6 Summary   12

2. Communication between Ada Programs   13
  2.1 The Operating System's Model of Concurrency   13
  2.2 The PULSE Inter-Program Communication Facility   15
    2.2.1 Design Aims   15
    2.2.2 Design Issues   16
      2.2.2.1 Process Naming   16
      2.2.2.2 Process Synchronisation   17
      2.2.2.3 The Representation of a Message   22
      2.2.2.4 Communication Failures   22
      2.2.2.5 Software Generated Interrupts   23
    2.2.3 Example Use of the IPC   24
  2.3 Evaluation of the PULSE IPC   26
  2.4 Summary   27

3. The PULSE Distributed File System   29
  3.1 Design Aims and Constraints   29
  3.2 The User's View   31

3.3 File System Architecture	32
3.3.1 File Replication	32
3.3.2 File System Object Naming	33
3.3.2.1 Master Volumes	34
3.3.2.2 Duplicate Volumes	34
3.3.2.3 I-number Allocation	35
3.3.2.4 Directories	35
3.3.3 File Location	36
3.3.4 Duplicate File Synchronisation	37
3.3.5 File Protection	38
3.4 User Control	38
3.4.1 File Selection Control	39
3.4.2 File Replication Control	40
3.5 The File Server as a Distributed Name Server	40
3.6 File Server Communication Protocols	41
3.7 Summary	42
4. The PULSE User Interface	**43**
4.1 Introduction	43
4.2 UNIX System Facilities	44
4.3 PULSE System Facilities	46
4.3.1 PULSE Kernel	46
4.3.2 File Server Operations	48
4.4 The Command Language	50
4.4.1 User Interaction	50
4.5 The UNIX and PULSE Command Interface	51
4.5.1 Initial Behaviour	53
4.5.2 UNIX Expression of Shell Commands	53
4.5.3 PULSE Expression of Shell Commands	57
4.6 Discussion of PULSE Shell Implementation	61
4.6.1 Tasking	61
4.6.2 Arguments	64
4.6.3 Performance	64
4.7 Summary	64
5. User Programming	**67**
5.1 System Packages	67
5.2 An Example Package	69
5.3 A Simple Example Tool	72
5.4 A Further Example Tool	72
5.5 An Example of a Distributed Program	79
5.6 Summary	81

6. The PULSE Kernel Implementation   83
  6.1 Introduction   83
  6.2 LSI-11/23   85
  6.3 Physical Device Drivers   85
    6.3.1 The Cambridge Ring Interface   85
  6.4 Support for Ada Tasking and Exception Handling   87
    6.4.1 Program Expansion   90
    6.4.2 Overlays   90
    6.4.3 Rendezvous Support   90
    6.4.4 Task Scheduling   92
    6.4.5 Exception Handling   92
    6.4.6 Limitations   93
  6.5 Inter-Program Communication (IPC)   93
    6.5.1 Mediums   93
    6.5.2 Messages and their Structure   94
    6.5.3 Reply and Transfer Medium   95
    6.5.4 Error Handling   95
    6.5.5 The Network Server   96
  6.6 Program Loading   97
  6.7 Logical Device Interface   99
  6.8 Current Status   99

7. The PULSE Distributed File System Implementation   101
  7.1 Introduction   101
  7.2 The Public Interface   102
    7.2.1 File Server Request Mediums   102
    7.2.2 Open File Mediums   102
    7.2.3 Reply Mediums   102
    7.2.4 Resource Deallocation   103
    7.2.5 Program Execution   103
    7.2.6 Distribution and Replication   104
  7.3 Implementation Constraints   105
    7.3.1 Ada Language Constraints   105
    7.3.2 Restrictions on Use of Tasking   105
      7.3.2.1 Task Storage Overhead   105
    7.3.3 Dynamic Storage Allocation   106
    7.3.4 Overlays   106
    7.3.5 Task Synchronisation Overhead   107
  7.4 File Server Structure   107
    7.4.1 Use of Tasking   107
  7.5 The Library High   109
    7.5.1 Open Files   110

7.6 The Library Low	111
7.6.1 The Disk Buffer Cache	113
7.6.1.1 Buffer Representation	113
7.6.1.2 Buffer Allocation	114
7.6.1.3 Physical I/O	114
7.6.1.4 Limits to Parallelism	114
7.6.1.5 Rendezvous Optimisation	115
7.6.2 Disk Volumes	115
7.6.2.1 Disk Volume Layout	115
7.6.2.2 Disk Volume Mounting	116
7.6.3 The Active I-node Level	116
7.6.3.1 Package Inode's User Interface	116
7.6.3.2 Duplicate File Synchronisation	117
7.6.3.3 I-node Table Manager Task	117
7.6.3.4 Remote Active I-nodes	118
7.6.3.5 Logical File I/O	119
7.6.3.6 The Private Interface	120
7.6.3.7 Communication Protocol	121
7.6.4 Directories	123
7.7 Statistics	124
7.8 Summary	125

8. Performance Evaluation   127

8.1 Performance Evaluation of the PULSE Kernel	127
8.1.1 Rendezvous Times	127
8.1.2 Overlay Times	128
8.1.3 Allocating and Deallocating Mediums	128
8.1.4 Basic Communication Overhead	129
8.1.5 Data Transaction Performance Figures	130
8.2 Distributed File System	134
8.2.1 File server operations	135
8.2.2 General Measurements	136
8.2.3 Interpretation of Measurements	138
8.2.4 Nassi-Habermann Optimisation	140
8.3 Summary	141

9. Retrospective   143

9.1 General Architecture	143
9.2 Using Ada	145
9.3 Distributed Programming	148
9.4 Closing Remarks	148

Appendix A: The Ada Representation of the PULSE IPC   151
Appendix B: PULSE Programmer's Manual Entries   161

Appendix C: A Review of Ada Tasking — 193
  C.1 The Tasking Model — 193
    C.1.1 Communication and Synchronisation — 194
    C.1.2 Task Types and Task Access Variables — 197
    C.1.3 Entry Family — 198
    C.1.4 Task Abortion — 198
    C.1.5 Task Attributes — 199
  C.2 Evaluation of the Rendezvous — 199
    C.2.1 Requirements for a Synchronisation Mechanism — 199
      C.2.1.1 Modularity — 199
      C.2.1.2 Expressive Power and Ease of Use — 200
    C.2.2 Bloom's Methodology Applied to Ada — 201
      C.2.2.1 Modularity Requirements — 201
      C.2.2.2 Expressive Power — 203
      C.2.2.3 Ease of Use — 210
  C.3 Conclusions — 227

References — 229
Index — 241

Preface

The PULSE distributed operating system was developed as part of a research programme in distributed systems carried out in the Department of Computer Science at the University of York during the period October 1979 to October 1984. Our initial efforts included the study of alternative methods of distributing the UNIX[1] operating system on several microprocessors connected by a fast local area network such as the Cambridge Ring. As a result we decided to concentrate on the design and implementation of a UNIX-like operating system for a network of powerful personal computers.

Other research interests in the department at the start of the project included the design of programming languages for embedded computer applications. Ian Wand, in particular, was involved both in the production of a Modula compiler and in the U.S. Department of Defense common programming language effort which resulted in the design of Ada.[2] Following the announcement that 'Ada was Green' an Ada compiler development project was established. Although the language is intended primarily for the programming of embedded computer systems, its application domain includes both general and distributed systems programming. The Ada language seemed a natural bridge between our project and the compiler project; consequently, we decided to use it to design and implement PULSE.

PULSE is one of the first projects to use Ada to implement an operating system. In this book we discuss the influence that Ada has had on its design, describe the structure of PULSE in detail and report on our experiences in its construction. The book is aimed primarily at workers in the field of distributed systems, especially those who may in the future consider Ada as an implementation vehicle. However, we hope that programmers who already find themselves faced with the task of producing systems in Ada will find much of interest. We assume that the reader has some familiarity with the Ada language, however, because PULSE makes extensive use of its parallel programming facilities, we include an appendix which reviews Ada tasking.

[1]UNIX is a trademark of AT&T.
[2]Ada is a registered trademark of the U.S. Government, Ada Joint Program Office.

In Chapter 1 we introduce the three main aspects of our work: distributed computing, the UNIX operating system and the Ada programming language. We discuss various approaches to distributing a UNIX-like system and present our model. An informal classification of distributed operating systems is given in order to place our work in a wider context.

The influence that Ada has had on our system and how it has been used in the inter-program communication facility is discussed in Chapter 2. In particular, we present a mechanism whereby independent Ada programs may communicate in a manner which is consistent with the inter-task communication found within a single Ada program.

In Chapter 3 we describe the architecture of the Distributed File System which provides a single global UNIX-like hierarchy with a consistent appearance when accessed from any machine. We also give details of our file replication scheme which improves reliability, increases performance and enables each machine to run either stand-alone or as a component of the distributed system.

In Chapter 4 the user interface is considered and the facilities provided by PULSE with those of UNIX are compared. We discuss how we provide a 'UNIX-like' command interface in terms of 'UNIX-unlike' system primitives. Chapter 5 then addresses user programming, and some of the software tools that have been written are described.

In Chapters 6 and 7 the implementations of the PULSE kernel and the PULSE Distributed File System are described. In particular we highlight the use and implementation of Ada tasking. Then, in Chapter 8, we give a performance evaluation of the prototype system.

The book concludes with a retrospective of the project. We also include three appendices: Appendix A contains the package specification of the inter-program communication facility, Appendix B is the PULSE Programmer's Manual, and in Appendix C we examine the tasking model and present some of the problems we have encountered in its use.

The project was initiated by Ian Wand; the early system design was done by Gerry Tomlinson and Andy Wellings and then refined and implemented with David Keeffe. The authors would like to thank Charles Forsyth for his help, particularly during the adaptation of his Ada run-time system for use in the PULSE kernel. We would also like to thank Ian Pyle for his support and Alan Burns for his contribution to our review of Ada tasking.

Acknowledgements

We gratefully acknowledge the receipt of two grants (GR/A/85889 and GR/B/78076) from the Distributed Computing Systems Panel of the Science and Engineering Research Council of Great Britain, which has funded the project. We would like to thank the coordinators of the DCS programme for their help throughout the project, particularly Rob Witty and David Duce. Our experimental system has involved extensive use of the York Ada Workbench Compiler. We would like to acknowledge all those involved in that project.

Much of the material found in this book is adapted from previous reports, papers written by the group and a D.Phil. thesis written by one of the authors. In particular, the following papers have been published or accepted for publication:

A. J. Wellings, G. M. Tomlinson, D. Keeffe, and I. C. Wand. (1984). Communication between Ada programs. *In* 'Conference on Ada Application and Environments' (15-18 October, St. Paul Minnesota), pp. 145-152. [copyright 1984 IEEE]

G. M. Tomlinson, D. Keeffe, I. C. Wand, and A. J. Wellings. (1985). The PULSE distributed file system. *In* 'Software—Practice and Experience.' Wiley, London. [in press]

D. Keeffe, G. M. Tomlinson, A. J. Wellings, and I. C. Wand. (accepted 1985). Aspects of Portability of the UNIX shell. *Proc. IEE (E)*, Computer and Digital Techniques. [in press]

A. J. Wellings, D. Keeffe, and G. M. Tomlinson. (1984). A problem with Ada and resource allocation. *ACM Ada Lett.* 3(4).

1 INTRODUCTION

The last few years have seen dramatic advances in computer technology which have led to increased performance, miniaturisation and a reduction in cost of computing equipment. When these advances are taken in conjunction with the development of effective communication media, we have the possibility of connecting many individual computer systems, often separated by great distances, which can collaborate and work towards a common goal. Such systems are usually called Distributed Systems and they introduce a number of specific technical problems into the system design. These problems include: general architecture, operating systems (including issues such as resource management, interprocess communication, synchronisation and atomic transactions), and a language suitable for the programming of such systems.

UNIX has recently emerged as a de facto industrial standard operating system. Ada is intended to be a standard concurrent programming language for developing real-time systems. The PULSE project attempts to take the best features of UNIX and apply them to a distributed environment using Ada as the implementation vehicle. By doing this we hope firstly to provide a distributed environment which amongst other things supports the development and execution of Ada programs, and secondly to show some of the problems that will be encountered in producing distributed systems in general and those written in Ada in particular.

Before discussing the specific issues addressed during the PULSE project, we will consider the advantages which a distributed system has over its non-distributed equivalents.

1.1 Distributed Computing

There are many motives for constructing distributed computer systems[65,46,28,51,66]; they include the following.

Performance

Although there have been significant improvements in the performance of processors due to technological advances, there are physical limits which govern the density to which switching and signalling components may be packed and the velocity at which signals may be sent[65]. Interconnecting several processor elements to co-operate on a single activity is therefore probably the only means of improving performance further[66].

Increased Availability and Reliability

The availability of a system is the probability that it will be able to service a given request[67]. The reliability of a system is a measure of the success with which it conforms to its specification without a failure[87]. A distributed system with decentralised control offers the potential of embedding redundancy into the hardware, the software and the data, in order that a failure in one component does not jeopardise the ability of the system as a whole. The general approach to achieving high availability and high reliability in a distributed system is based therefore on the tolerance of faults rather than their avoidance.

Extensibility

The extensibility or modularity of a system is the degree to which its performance and functionality can be changed without changing the system design. Jensen remarks:

"Distributed computer systems appear to offer extensibility improvements over these configurations, [that is uniprocessors and networks] due to decentralisation of the interconnection and control logic (both hardware and software). As a system is scaled up or down in size, nonlinearities and boundary conditions in performance are less likely than for centralised systems. Thus, it is feasible to specify minimum and maximum system sizes, together with the number and size of the increments between, to meet the application requirements. It is also more probable that the additional functionality and performance of each increment can be incorporated without hardware and software design changes."[51]

Resource Sharing

There are several resources which may be provided for computer users; they include general programming services, specialist programs, large centralised databases and specialist peripherals. A large organisation may have many computer systems but be unable to provide all resources on every one. Distributed systems provide a means by which these resources can be shared.

Geographical Separation

In areas of real time systems, such as process control, and office automation, it is important to have processor power available where it is required. However, it is also necessary for these processors to communicate and co-operate. Distributed systems provide an environment where both requirements may be satisfied.

Clarity

Many problems are of a parallel nature and it may be awkward to express solutions within sequential algorithms.

1.1.1 Distributed System Definition

There have been many definitions of a distributed systems. PULSE most closely fits that given by Enslow who defines a "Fully Distributed Processing System"[27] as being distinguished by the following characteristics:

1) multiplicity of general resources, including processors;

2) loosely coupled physical interconnection;

3) a unity of control in that the system must define and support a unified set of policies governing its operation;

4) system transparency - users must be able to request services without being aware of their physical location; and

5) component autonomy - components operate in an autonomous fashion requiring cooperation with other components to exchange information.

1.2 The UNIX Operating System

UNIX[92] is a time-sharing system particularly suitable for program development and text processing. Although it is only in recent years that it has received widespread commercial use, it is not a new operating system and has been used extensively in Universities and research institutions since the early 1970s. We can do no better than quote Kernighan and Pike to explain the attractions of UNIX.

> "Even though the UNIX system introduces a number of innovative programs and techniques, no single program or idea makes it work well. Instead, what makes it effective is an approach to programming, a philosophy of using the computer. Although the philosophy can't be written down in a single sentence, at its heart is the idea that the power of the system comes more from the relationship between programs than from the programs themselves. Many UNIX programs do quite trivial tasks in isolation, but, combined with other programs, become general and useful tools."[61]

1.2.1 The File System

The most important role of UNIX, according to Ritchie and Thompson[92], is to provide a file system. It is central to the success of UNIX and is one of the best examples of the "keep it simple" philosophy which pervades the system's design.

The basic structure of the file system is a tree (which may span several devices) with the branches being directories and the leaves being files. Any file can be accessed by its name, either relative to some working directory or absolutely starting from the root of the tree. The latter name of a file is termed its pathname. Users can change their current position in the tree (i.e their current working directory). There is also a protection mechanism to prevent unauthorised access to files.

According to Kernighan and Mashey[58] there were two major design decisions which have resulted in the file system being so powerful and easy to use.

1   Directories are Files.

    The only distinction is that directories may be altered only by the system itself, because they contain information about the physical structure of the file system. Since directories are files they may be read by normal programs.

2   A File is just a Sequence of Bytes.

    As far as the system is concerned a file has no internal structure.

- There are no tracks or cylinders; the system conceals the physical characteristics of devices.

- There are no physical or logical records or associated counts (and therefore no fixed/variable length distinction and no blocking); the only bytes in the file are those put there by the user.

- There is no preallocation of file space; a file is as big as it needs to be.

- There is no distinction between random and sequential access; the bytes of a file are accessible in any order.

As Kernighan and Mashey[58] point out these are not deficiencies, but are major contributions to the effectiveness of the system. Files can have structure but that structure is imposed by user programs not by the system. Archives and object modules are good examples.

Access Permissions

Each file has a set of access permissions associated with it, which determine the access rights of the owner, users in the same group as the owner, and others. Each of these can have read, write and execute permissions.

1.2.2 The UNIX Process Model

New processes are created using the "fork" primitive which creates a child process whose code and data are identical to that of the parent. The child inherits the open files of the parent and executes concurrently with it. The child and parent can determine their identities and the parent may wait for its children to terminate. Furthermore, communication between related processes can be achieved via a buffered channel, called a pipe, using the standard file system operations for reading and writing.

1.3 The Ada Programming Language

One of the most important features of UNIX is the use of a high-level language to implement the system. Ada[23] was chosen as the implementation language for PULSE for the following reasons.

1) The Department of Computer Science had been involved in the development of the language and was in the process of writing an Ada compiler[85].

2) We felt that Ada was likely to be the most important systems implementation language of the next decade and were interested to explore and evaluate it as it developed.

3) There was a lack of any suitable alternative which offered higher-level constructs other than those found in C[59], the standard UNIX implementation language. In particular we wanted a concurrent programming language

with encapsulation facilities. Languages such as extended CLU[70,72,71,73,74], Mesa[77], Modula-2[111], and PLITS[30] were unavailable to us.

The following features of Ada, taken from Barnes[6], were seen to be advantageous to the project.

Readability

> The language is designed so that programs written in Ada may be more easily read and therefore more easily maintained and modified than programs in other, terser languages.

Strong Typing

> Strong typing enables many programming errors to be detected during compilation.

Programming in the Large

> The language provides mechanisms for encapsulation, separate compilation and library management which aid the programming of large complicated systems.

Exception Handling

> The language provides a means whereby the consequence of run-time errors can be contained.

Data abstraction

> By separating the details of data from the specification of the logical operations on the data, the language promotes portability and maintainability.

Tasking

> An important characteristic inherent in distributed systems is that many activities proceed in parallel. Consequently individual programs on such systems are themselves likely to need to express concurrency. By providing linguistic support programs can become less complex, and hence more reliable. The Ada tasking model is described and reviewed in appendix C.

Generic Units

> In many cases the logical section of a program is independent of the type of data on which it operates. Generic units in the language provide a mechanism from which several related sections of programs can be created from a single template.

Had we found it necessary to change the language to make it more suitable for distributed systems, we had thought that we could change our compiler. However, it became clear due to the complexity of Ada that this was not practical. Consequently we have made no changes to the language whatsoever.

1.4 The PULSE Distributed Operating System

In the previous sections we have attempted to give our view as to why UNIX is a suitable starting point from which to build our distributed operating system. We have not mentioned any on the criticisms of UNIX although they are many and varied and we have not set out to remedy any of its limitations.

We are concerned with building a UNIX-like system so it is only necessary here to define the features of UNIX proper which we would retain in our system. These are:

1) a hierarchical file store with demountable volumes and the ability to access devices as files,

2) the dynamic creation of processes at the user level,

3) standard input/output with pipes linking programs,

4) the user interface and the availability of software tools, and

5) the system written in a high-level language.

1.4.1 Methods of Distribution

We considered four distinct methods of constructing our distributed system.

The first has a central machine, which handles all calls on the operating system, and small satellite processors each of which runs a single process. Work in this area has been done by Barak and Shapip[5], Karshmer[57], Tanenbaum[99] and at Bell Laboratories[75].

The second distributes the operating system functions between each of the processors. In such a system one still allocates a single process per processor but each processor has the ability to communicate with every other one.

The third has several processes per processor. Processes are allocated to processors at process creation time and may even migrate to achieve load balancing[19].

The fourth is based upon the concept of a personal computer, where each such computer has a single user who may run one or more programs concurrently on the machine. There are a variety of system architectures based on this model.

One possibility is to grant the user sole access to a processor when logging in, as in the Cambridge Distributed System[110,39,81]. In this system, terminals are not directly connected to the personal computers but to concentrators which multiplex terminal I/O traffic on the local area network. This method has advantages when the distributed system offers a range of machines with different capabilities. However, no useful work is possible if the network is not operational.

A second possibility is for all computers to have a terminal and disks directly connected allowing a user to work, possibly in a restricted manner, independently of the network. The network is used only for communication between machines for the sharing of expensive resources, such as quality printers and mass disk storage. This can be compared with the Xerox PARC model[90,47,68,113,76] for office automation and the Carnegie-Mellon model for a scientific interactive computing environment[24,89,1,94,20].

This second approach was adopted as the overall architecture for the PULSE system.

1.4.2 Ada and Distributed Systems

One approach to designing a distributed operating system in Ada is to consider it as a single program distributed across the network. However, the Ada language has been found unsuitable for this environment[106]. The main problems are connected with the use of shared variables between tasks on processors without shared memory[26,97], the absence of a suitable language construct to represent a node in the network[53,52], the difficulty in implementing the rendezvous in a distributed system where there are processor and network failures[91], and the inability to express all possible constraints on synchronisation using the rendezvous primitives (See appendix C).

Alternatively an operating system may be viewed as a collection of co-operating Ada programs. Although the language itself does not recognise that more than one Ada program may co-operate towards a single goal (unlike the Mesa language[77] where separate programs may be bound together dynamically), the programming support environment[22] does recognise the need for co-operating tools, written in Ada, which may be required in the development of Ada programs.

The Ada Language Reference Manual defines a standard environment in which programs execute. This environment is provided by a library package which is accessible to all Ada programs. When implementing the PULSE Distributed Operating System, facilities were introduced into the environment so that independent Ada programs can communicate. The operating system is a collection of such programs distributed across the network. These "server" programs provide an extensible set of services which may be requested by "client" programs via the inter-program communication facility.

All programs are supported by a basic kernel at each node in the network. The kernel supports tasking and exception handling for a number of Ada programs executing in separate address spaces. It also provides mechanisms for inter-program communication and program execution, and access to local physical devices including the network. Each node also runs an instance of the PULSE file server program, which by co-operating with its partners on other nodes, implements the PULSE Distributed File System.

1.5 Distributed Operating Systems

In order to place PULSE in a wider context, there follows an informal classification of distributed operating systems.

o   Network of Autonomous Systems with the Network Visible

   The main characteristic of this class is that the network is used explicitly. No attempt is made to hide the underlying system from the user. In order that machines of widely differing architectures, and usually different operating systems, may communicate, there must be protocols for all projected activities. One such system is 'uucp'[82], whereby different UNIX systems may transfer files; another is represented by certain implementations of the "Blue Book" file transfer protocol[36]. At command level of both these systems the user must express the communication in terms of "machine name" and "operation name". The user must know the "address" of the remote machine. Such systems are said to have "unrelated naming domains"[112].

o   Network of Autonomous Systems with the Network Hidden

   Systems within this category are similar to those described above, except that the presence of a network is hidden from the user. This is usually achieved by introducing a suitable layer of software between the user and the network. A feature of these systems is that the user must know the location of the resource within his name space, but he may not know whether that name denotes a remote or local object. It does not follow that the name space for the overall "super-system" appears the same from different points within it, with the possible result that a resource may have different names from different nodes in the network. Such systems are said to have "adjoining naming domains"[112]. Examples that fall within this category are the National Software Works[42], the Newcastle Connection[15], and Cocanet[93].

o   Loosely Coupled Systems with Autonomous Nodes

This category is characterised by the presentation of a uniform name space to all users, but where individual nodes of the system may function alone, albeit with only a subset of that name space available to them. Any given resource will have the same name, irrespective of the source of the request. Additionally, the name may denote a resource which, depending on circumstances, may be either local or remote. Such systems are said to have a "single naming domain"[112]. PULSE may be placed in this category, along with the LOCUS Distributed Operating System[84]

o   Loosely Coupled Systems with Non-autonomous Nodes

Systems within this division are similar to those in the previous one, except that the nodes are not capable of operating alone. A machine removed from the network will no longer be operable, but the remainder will continue to function. Examples are Arachne[96], the New Mexico State University (NMSU) Ring-Star system[57], UNIX with Satellite Processors[5] and several others[99,81,16].

o   Tightly Coupled Distributed Systems

Unlike the systems described above, this category applies to several processors sharing memory on a common bus. One such system is StarOS[56]; there are others.

The categories above are not exhaustive; for example no attempt has been made to categorise the network nodes themselves. That is, no mention is made of the homogeneity or power of the processors, or whether there is local file storage.

1.6 Summary

PULSE is an experimental distributed operating system for a network of powerful personal computers. Its main features are its ability to operate both connected to and independently of the network, and its hierarchical file system. It is written in Ada and provides support for several Ada programs executing in separate address spaces at each node.

2 COMMUNICATION BETWEEN ADA PROGRAMS

In this chapter we discuss the influence that Ada has had on our system: in particular we examine the mechanism in PULSE by which independent Ada programs intercommunicate.

Throughout this chapter the term process is used to denote a sequence of actions performed by executing a sequence of instructions on a real or virtual processor. When discussing general principles we use the term process, when discussing processes in Ada we use the term task, and when describing an executing Ada program which consists of several tasks sharing the same address space we use the term program.

2.1 The Operating System's Model of Concurrency

Having decided that the distributed operating system should be structured as a set of separate but co-operating Ada programs, the next consideration is what influence the Ada model of concurrency should have on the operating system's model of concurrency. Taking UNIX as the starting point three alternatives were considered:

1) The Ada model can be ignored and the UNIX 'fork and execute' model implemented by the operating system, which itself would be written in a sequential subset of Ada. Any multi-tasking in a user's Ada program would be invisible to the operating system. A local run-time support system would be necessary to map an Ada task onto a UNIX process.

This approach was rejected because the UNIX process model and the Ada tasking model are so different that no operating system concurrency could be exploited in a single multi-tasked Ada program. To obtain concurrency the user would have to create several system processes, each of which would be viewed by the operating system as a separate program and would therefore run in its own protected address space. Communication between these processes would use an inter-program communication facility defined by the operating system.

However, an advantage of this approach is that a wide range of languages can be supported, each being able to create new processes; to adopt any particular language's concurrency philosophy may result in programs in other languages having difficulty in creating new processes. This general approach has been adopted by the Spice project[24] where the Accent kernel[89] supports mechanisms for process creation and inter-program communication. A variety of languages are supported; however, any concurrency in a language, such as Ada, is invisible to the Accent kernel and must be supported by a local run-time system.

2) This approach is similar to the first, except the operating system itself is written in multi-task Ada. However, the Ada tasking model is not the model of concurrency presented to the user: this remains the UNIX model. The Tunis[44] operating system adopts a similar approach with Concurrent Euclid[45] as the implementation language.

This approach was rejected for the same reasons as that above.

3) The UNIX process model may be replaced completely. Both the operating system and the user's programs would use Ada tasking and would share a common run-time support system. As in 1 and 2 above the complete programs would run in protected address spaces; however, tasks within the programs would be scheduled individually and independently. Programs in other languages would be treated by the operating system as single task Ada programs; any program with its own parallel processing features would be handled by a local run-time support system.

The third approach is adopted by the PULSE Distributed Operating System since it can best exploit the tasking features of Ada. It can be compared with the Pilot[90] operating system which is written in Mesa[77]. However, in that system both user programs and the operating system run in a single virtual address space - no other language is allowed. In a sense, all of Pilot can be thought of as a very powerful run-time support package for the Mesa Language[90]. Similarly PULSE is based on Ada, and the run-time support required for Ada tasking is provided by the PULSE kernel.

2.2 The PULSE Inter-Program Communication Facility

Inter-process communication is fundamental to any distributed operating system. In PULSE, this is made more complex by the existence of two modes of concurrency: besides the expected communication between tasks in a given program, programs themselves need some means of communication. Intra-program communication is provided by the rendezvous: inter-program communication (IPC) uses the extra facilities introduced into a program's environment.

2.2.1 Design Aims

The IPC facility was designed with the following aims:

1) To allow programs to communicate using the current language primitives, including those for selecting different communication options and for timing out. However we did not want to change the language or provide special compiler support.

2) To provide uniform access to user and kernel resources both local and remote. As PULSE is an experimental system, it is desirable to be able to move resources in and out of the kernel to experiment with efficiency trade-offs. Furthermore the mechanisms for sending and receiving a message should be the same irrespective of whether that program is local or remote. However, this does not necessarily imply that the network is completely invisible to the user program. For example it may need to be aware that a message to a remote program may not be delivered and wish to use a timeout when waiting for a reply.

3) To allow one program to transfer the ability to communicate to another. We wish to be able to set up arbitrary communication paths dynamically between independent programs.

2.2.2 Design Issues

There are four issues which dominate message-based communication[32]: process naming, process synchronisation, the representation of a message and the handling of communication failures. The design of the PULSE IPC facility is now considered taking each of these issues into account.

2.2.2.1 Process Naming

A common form of process interaction in a distributed operating system is the client-server relationship where a server provides services for several clients: a method is required by which these clients can identify a particular server. Processes may name each other directly, or indirectly through some intermediary. Clearly a direct naming scheme along the lines of CSP[41] is unsuitable as a server would have to be aware of all possible clients. Ada's naming scheme, where a called task is unaware of the identity of the caller, has contributed to problems with the rendezvous when task failures occur[107]. Furthermore, with a direct naming scheme it is not possible for many readers to receive messages from many writers. The PULSE IPC therefore provides an indirect naming scheme. However, rather than naming a passive intermediary, such as a Link[96] or a Port[89], a program names a buffer task, termed a "Medium", which has entries for sending and receiving messages; such tasks are part of the run-time support and reside in the kernel.

This scheme has the advantage that it enables communication between tasks in separate Ada programs to be achieved using the same mechanisms as communication between tasks in a single Ada program, thereby achieving the first aim of the IPC. The disadvantage is that it views both sending and receiving of messages as entry calls.

Although many different programs may write to the same Medium, the asymmetry of the rendezvous means that it is not possible for a single reader task to wait for a message from more than one Medium at once. This restriction can be overcome by introducing a further task between each Medium and the receiving task.

As programs may reside on different nodes in the network it is simpler to allow a Medium only a single reader for the following reasons:

1) No dialogue is required between reader programs across the network as there is no competition for messages.

2) A message need be stored only at a single site in the network - that of the reader.

The main disadvantage of this is that it is obviously not possible to have several server programs satisfying a number of clients. The PULSE IPC therefore allows only one Ada program to read from a Medium but allows any task within that program to access it. It is the responsibility of the program designer to prevent two tasks accidently accessing the same Medium. This protection may be implemented using the scope rules of the Ada language. Allowing only a single reader program, but many reader tasks, gives the benefit of parallelism without the complications of the general case of many-readers and many-writers.

Mediums are defined by a task type in the IPC package which also contains subprograms for their creation and destruction. When a program creates a Medium the system returns a variable whose task type is defined by "access Medium". This variable is the program's local identity of the Medium and may be considered as a capability to access that Medium. As programs cannot name Mediums directly they cannot accidently reference Mediums for which they have no capability. The added protection has the overhead that the kernel must keep a mapping of local identities to global identities. The kernel must also be involved when Medium capabilities are transferred from one program to the other.

2.2.2.2 Process Synchronisation

Having decided that communication between programs should be via a Medium task residing in the operating system kernel we must consider what form of synchronisation should be provided. Liskov[71] has suggested three possibilities: the no-wait send, the synchronised send and the remote invocation send. We now present how they may variously be incorporated into possible implementations of Mediums.

1) The No-Wait Send.

In Figure 2.1 the sender continues execution immediately the message has been sent to the Medium. Each Medium task has a queue associated with it, which is controlled by the package message_manager, itself an instantiation of a generic package for queue manipulation. The routines queue, unqueue, queue_full and queue_empty are provided by that package.

When the queue is not full, the Medium will accept an entry call to send a message. When the queue is not empty, the Medium will accept a call to receive a message. Flow control is thereby provided by blocking the sending task when the queue is full.

```ada
task type medium is
  entry send_message(mess : in message);
  entry receive_message(mess : in out message);
end medium;

task body medium is
  package message_manager is
            new queue(QUEUE_LENGTH,message);
begin
  loop
    select
      when not message_manager.queue_full =>
        accept send_message(mess : in message) do
          message_manager.queue(mess);
        end send_message;
    or
      when not message_manager.queue_empty =>
        accept receive_message(mess : in out message) do
          mess := message_manager.unqueue;
        end receive_message;
    end select;
  end loop;
end medium;
```

Figure 2.1: The No-Wait Send Medium

2) The Synchronised Send.

In Figure 2.2 the sender waits until the message has been received. The Medium task holds the sender in the rendezvous until the receiver has made the "receive" entry call. All other senders are blocked at the "send" entry.

```
task type medium is
  entry send_message(in_mess : in message);
  entry receive_message(out_mess : in out message);
end medium;

task body medium is
begin
  loop
    accept send_message(in_mess : in message) do
      accept receive_message(out_mess : in out message) do
        out_mess := in_mess;
      end receive_message;
    end send_message;
  end loop;
end medium;
```

Figure 2.2: The Synchronised Send Medium

3) The Remote Invocation Send.

In Figure 2.3 the sender waits until it has received a reply. The sender is held in the rendezvous until the receiver has both received the message and sent a reply.

```
task type medium is
  entry send_message(in_mess1 : in message;
                     reply_mess : in out message);
  entry receive_message(out_mess : in out message);
  entry send_reply(in_mess2 : in message);
end medium;

task body medium is
begin
  loop
    accept send_message(in_mess1 : in message;
                        reply_mess : in out message) do
      accept receive_message(out_mess : in out message) do
        out_mess := in_mess1;
      end receive_message;
      accept send_reply(in_mess2 : in message) do
        reply_mess := in_mess2;
      end send_reply;
    end send_message;
  end loop;
end medium;
```

Figure 2.3: The Remote Invocation Send Medium

The Remote Invocation Send is the mechanism closest to the Ada rendezvous, and thus seems the most appropriate, but has two disadvantages. Firstly, the receiving program may be on another machine and there may be a significant delay before a reply is received. Forcing the sender to wait may reduce potential parallelism unless further tasks are created. Unfortunately there is a high overhead associated with an Ada task, especially at creation time, so unnecessary dynamic creation should be avoided. Secondly, as Liskov[71] points out, not all message exchanges are of this form. In particular a reply message may come from a different program from that which received the original message. For example, a request to a program to print a file may result in a message to the first available printer server which would then reply when the printing had finished. In the Thoth operating system[17] a transfer facility is provided to enable the receiver of a message to transfer it to a further process while still blocking the sender. This approach was rejected because there is no equivalent facility provided by the rendezvous mechanism.

The Synchronised Send avoids the need for buffering but again reduces parallelism. The No-Wait send is the most flexible and it is this that was adopted for the PULSE IPC. Programs which require the synchronised or remote invocation send may build them from the no-wait send primitive.

To send or receive a message a task makes an entry call on a Medium. Conditional and timed entry calls may be used for greater flexibility. For example, to receive a message only if it is immediately available a task would use the following conditional entry call:

```
select
    from_medium.receive_message(mess);
else
    -- do something else
end select;
```

Similarly with a timed entry call,

```
select
    from_medium.receive_message(mess);
or
    delay 10.0;
end select;
```

the calling task will wait for the specified period before proceeding.

The conditional and timed entry calls on sending a message can be used to withdraw from communication when a Medium's queue is full. This provides an alternative mechanism for flow control to that provided automatically by the "no-wait send" Medium. Had the synchronised send been chosen, then the timed "send" entry call would enable the sending task to time out if the Medium were unavailable for conveying the message, however, once the message was in transit no timeout would be possible. Furthermore, for the remote invocation send, once a message had been received by the Medium the sender would have been blocked until the reply had been received. A parameter to the send would be necessary to allow this extra level of timeout.

2.2.2.3 The Representation of a Message

The Ada compiler has no knowledge of the PULSE IPC, which is supported solely by the environment in which the programs execute. Consequently only messages of a known type, such as bytes, characters, integers, boolean and floats can be transmitted. The message is expressed in Ada as a variant record whose discriminant denotes the type of data to be sent. The actual data is held in a variable length array of that type. All messages have a header portion which contains a reply Medium descriptor, a transfer Medium descriptor and a user-supplied integer for reference.

In practice these facilities are not sufficient; a number of record structures have also been included to allow an efficient implementation of the file system. Also the concept of "unsafe data" transfer has been introduced to allow variable length and variable typed data to be received.

2.2.2.4 Communication Failures

The PULSE distributed operating system is designed to operate over a local area network. Whilst these networks are not error-free they do have significantly lower error rates than wide area networks; for example the Cambridge Ring has an error rate of 1 in 5×10^{11} [80]. Consequently the PULSE IPC uses a lightweight network protocol thereby allowing higher level programs to obtain optimum bandwidth. The IPC provides a simple virtual circuit[21] in that it maintains the connection between two programs and it guarantees that messages received will be in good condition and in sequence*. However, it does not guarantee that messages will arrive. Any error from programs communicating result in the kernel raising an exception in those programs. We must consider two classes of error.

1) Errors which occur due to a failure of a processing node in the network or in the underlying communication subsystem.

---

*These facilities come cheaply in local area networks.

If a connection fails an exception is raised when the reader or writer attempts to access the Medium. This enables a server program to deallocate resources dedicated to the service of client programs regardless of how they terminate.

If an important message is sent, then the sender will probably expect to receive an acknowledgement or a reply. Failure may occur because the original message or the reply has been lost. There are two reasons for such loss: the first is when no message can be sent on the reply Medium because the connection has been broken. In this case an exception is raised by the Medium inside the "receive_message" rendezvous. This exception is propagated to the calling task. The second possibility is that a message has been lost but the connection is not broken. In this case a timeout can be associated with the reply message. If it has not been received during this period, the message can be sent again. Higher level protocols such as repeatable[78] or atomic[50] transactions can be left to further layers of software.

2) Errors due to invalid attempts at communication.

For example a program might issue an entry call to a Medium for which it does not have a valid capability. Ideally, such an error would be caught during compilation by having constrained access to a Medium task. Unfortunately this is not possible in Ada, so an exception must be raised at run-time. Another exception is raised when the receiving task tries to receive a message which is of different type to the one expected.

2.2.2.5 Software Generated Interrupts

The IPC is for programs which are expecting to communicate: however, it must be possible for one program to communicate an event to another when that program is not expecting any communication to take place. For example it must be possible to abort an erroneous program. Rather than providing a general-purpose signal mechanism like that found in the UNIX operating system[92], we have allowed the Ada "abort" facility to be invoked asynchronously. A "break" exception, which is not as severe as abort in that it can be suppressed, but cannot be handled, is also provided. This approach was inspired by the Thoth operating system[17]. We have not yet investigated the possibility of using interrupt entries to handle such asynchronous communication.

2.2.3 Example Use of the IPC

Figure 2.4 presents a fragment of Ada which illustrates a possible use for the PULSE IPC. It shows a function to implement reliable message-sending - "reliable" here means that either messages are guaranteed to be delivered, or the sender is informed that the transaction has failed. In Liskov's terms, we are providing a remote invocation send, in that the sending task cannot continue until a reply has arrived. Furthermore we assume that all transactions are repeatable[78]. The possible outcomes are that the message has been sent and a reply received, or the destination is too busy to handle it or does not exist. These are the members of the type "result". The function is supplied with the message itself, the Medium through which it is transmitted, and the corresponding information to enable the reply to be received.

The routine uses timeouts and a maximum number of retries to determine success. Essentially the main (outer) loop sends a message and then waits for a reply; if none arrives within the timeout period (here 20 seconds) the retry count is incremented and the loop repeats. In Ada terms the inner loop works as follows. The timed "select" implements the timeout. Within the "success" arm of the select statement, the received message's reference number is checked against that of the sent message: if they do not match the message is discarded.

If at any time the IPC rendezvous fail, one of the two exceptions "NO_READER" or "NO_WRITER" is raised. In either case the destination is deemed to be or have become absent. Failure in other cases is deemed to be caused by the destination being too busy. The reference number in the messages is used to prevent the results of one call of reliable_send affecting subsequent calls: the number is incremented each time the function is used, so that replies arriving from previous use are discarded. The receiving routine is expected to copy this reference number from the incoming message into the reply.

```
type result is (MESS_SENT, DEST_BUSY, DEST_ABSENT);

use IPC;

function reliable_send(request     : p_message_t;
                      request_med : medium; reply  : p_message_t;
                      reply_med   : medium) return result is

   RETRY_COUNT : constant integer := 2;
begin

   request.my_ref := request.my_ref + 1;

   for i in 0 .. RETRY_COUNT loop
      request_med.send_message(request);
      loop
         select
            reply_med.receive_message(reply);
            if reply.my_ref = request.my_ref then
               return MESS_SENT;
            else
               -- ignore message
            end if;
         or
            delay 20.0;
            exit;          -- to retry
         end select;
      end loop;
   end loop;

   return DEST_BUSY;

exception
   when NO_READER or NO_WRITER =>
      return DEST_ABSENT;
end reliable_send;
```

Figure 2.4: Reliable Message-Sending

2.3 Evaluation of the PULSE IPC

The IPC was designed with three major aims, presented in Section 2.1. These aims have been achieved by providing a communication facility based on a buffer task. User and kernel resources are accessed via the IPC although for efficiency some messages to the kernel are implemented as procedural entries. The ability to pass Medium identifiers in messages, however, has only been partially successful; we have not yet addressed the problems of sending read capabilities across the network.

More generally Liskov[72] has suggested four properties that a communication primitive should provide.

1) User programs need not deal with the underlying form of messages. For example, users should not need to translate data into bit strings suitable for transmission, or to break up the message into packets.

2) All messages received by user programs are intact and in good condition. For example, if messages are broken into packets, then the system only delivers a message if all packets arrive at the receiving node, and are properly reassembled. Furthermore, if the bits in a message have been scrambled, the message either is not delivered, or is reconstructed before delivery; clearly some redundant information is required.

3) Messages received by a process are the kind that process expects. Support for this property requires type checking which may be performed either at compile time or run time.

4) Processes are not restricted to communicating only using a predefined set of types, e.g. the built-in ones. Instead, they can communicate in terms of values of interest to the application.

Of these four properties the PULSE IPC satisfies the first three: the fourth requires compiler support. This is a major limitation. In the implementation of the PULSE

Distributed File System (see chapters 3 and 7) it was found to be essential to communicate using data defined by the user's programs, not the kernel. Whilst an interface could have been produced which took a data structure and broke it down into kernel supported components, it was felt that the cost involved in assembling and disassembling the data would be too high. Consequently new built-in types were added. An alternative approach would have been to transfer all messages as "unsafe data" and rely on user programs to provide their own type security. For example, type secure communication may be achieved by having all communicating programs reference a common package which defines both the type and a user defined identifier for that type. On receipt of a message the identifier received could be compared with the identifier expected. Whilst this has the advantage that it requires no compiler support, its disadvantage is that the conversion between the type and the "unsafe data" must be done by the user.

2.4 Summary

We have developed a mechanism by which independent Ada programs may communicate using the Ada rendezvous. We have not made any changes to the language and we have not relied on any compiler support or implementation dependent pragmas for our basic concepts.

The IPC has been used extensively in the implementation of the PULSE Distributed Filing System and a number of system utilities. It has proved simple to use and a natural extension to the internal tasking facility. However, the fact that both sending and receiving a message are expressed as entry calls causes some awkwardness in programming style. The ability to apply a guard on the reception of a message, in the same manner as that applied to internal task communication, would undoubtedly be more pleasant. This is impossible due to the asymmetric nature of Ada task communication, and must be simulated by introducing a further buffer task within the receiving program. Furthermore, we have found that being able to transfer user defined record structures with type checking to be essential if programs are to co-operate safely towards a common goal.

3 THE PULSE DISTRIBUTED FILE SYSTEM

A major component of PULSE is its distributed file system, which combines individual machines' disk storage into a single UNIX-like hierarchical file store. This chapter describes the architecture of the distributed file system, discusses some implementation issues, and presents an example of the file system's ability to aid the building of higher level distributed software.

3.1 Design Aims and Constraints

In any network of computers, communication between machines is typically used to transfer files, exchange electronic mail, and allow access to particular peripherals. In a local area network, the communication overhead between machines is typically so low that extensive use is made of such facilities: some systems, such as the Cambridge Distributed System[81], even incorporate machines with no local disk storage. However, when the network is one of personal computers, the ability to access files locally offers the possibility of performance gains and the ability to run stand-alone. To achieve this, each machine must at least have copies of files containing system programs. This introduces the administrative problem of ensuring that changes to files are propagated to each machine in the network. Furthermore, users may have to struggle to communicate with several independent file systems. One way to overcome such problems is to provide an integrated distributed file system supporting network transparency and replication.

Network transparency, as provided in recent systems such as the Newcastle Connection[15] and Cocanet[93], enables user programs to reference files without regard to their location, with inter-machine communication being carried out on their behalf when necessary. Such a technique reduces the problems involved in machine communication: for instance a file may be copied from one machine to another in exactly the same way as within a single machine.

The replication of resources such as files is desirable to increase both availability and performance. This may obviously be achieved in an ad hoc manner by providing a similar environment (in terms of files available) on each machine. However if a replicated file is modified, then the change must be propagated to other sites by explicit copying. Support for replication at a low level overcomes these problems. In this case, instead of each machine having an independent file system, a single file system may be considered to be distributed across many machines.

The PULSE Distributed File System attempts to provide both network transparency and replication in a simple manner, taking regard of the particular characteristics of a personal computer network used primarily for program development. These include the following.

1) Users may freely connect and disconnect (both logically and physically) their personal computers to and from the network. Useful work must be possible whilst disconnected, i.e. running stand-alone.

2) Each machine has enough disk capacity to store most of its user's own files and enough system files to enable it to run stand-alone. However it typically has only a fraction of the capacity required to store copies of the complete file system.

3) Removable disks may be transported between machines.

Replication is supported at the level of individual files, as in systems such as LOCUS[84] and the Keele Distributed Filestore[8]. The existence of several copies of a file is hidden from the user at the highest level of the system. Moreover, since both directories and unstructured data files are replicated, the same (logical) file may be accessed using the same name from any machine in the network.

Thus in the terminology of Wupit[112], PULSE aims to provide a "single naming domain".

3.2 The User's View

The PULSE file system supports the notion of a "user" and associated file protection as in UNIX[92]. The user sees the PULSE file store as a single rooted tree of files, the non-terminal nodes of which are directories, the terminal nodes unstructured data files. Each file is uniquely identified by its absolute pathname, but may be referenced relative to a working directory. Any program invoked by reference to a remote file will run on the user's own machine but may communicate with programs running on other machines. Access to files is network transparent, in that neither the user nor the programs he invokes make any network-specific references.

The "view of the world" presented to a user is the same, whether or not he is connected to the network. All that the user sees and manipulates is expressed in terms of this file system, and it is this that is uniform, in that a given file will have the same absolute pathname at every point in the network.

The operations available are similar to those of a centralised UNIX system, augmented with a few distribution control primitives. The user may control the replication of files (including directories). He may ensure that a copy of a subset of the global file hierarchy (including the root) is kept locally on his machine. His choice of subset will depend upon the files he wishes to access when running stand-alone, the files he wishes to access at high speed, and his local disk capacity. He may change the subset, when, for instance, his machine's disk capacity changes. He may also choose to have copies of his files replicated at other sites to increase their availability. In particular, he may wish to have copies at a site which backs up its files to tape or other long term storage.

3.3 File System Architecture

We now discuss some of the problems involved in achieving the aims outlined above, and explain the file system architecture in some detail.

3.3.1 File Replication

As soon as a file system allows multiple copies of the same (logical) file to exist on different machines, it is faced with the problem of keeping them mutually consistent: a situation must not be allowed to arise whereby independent conflicting modifications have been made to different copies of the same file. In our personal computer network this problem is compounded by the freedom given to sites to withdraw from the network, regardless of the possibility of network partition due to machine or network failure. Fortunately the very nature of such a network allows us to make the assumption that most file modifications will be performed on a user's own machine. In this situation we consider the merits of a primary copy strategy[2] to outweigh the complexities of more sophisticated approaches such as voting[100,33] or version vectors[83].

In the PULSE distributed file system one particular copy of a single logical file is termed the "master copy", and only this copy may be modified directly. Any other copies are termed "duplicate copies" and may only be accessed for reading. When a file is opened, either directly in response to a client's "open" request or indirectly such as for a directory search or during program loading, the file system selects a particular copy of the requested file. Any further operations are performed on that copy. If the file is opened for writing then the master copy is always chosen, so that modifications are automatically directed to it. If it is unavailable then the attempted access is denied.

This method is similar to that proposed for the Spice file system[102], the major difference being that PULSE provides a single naming domain for files and hence replicates directories as well as unstructured data files. Unlike the system proposed by Alsberg and Day[2], it is not possible to elect a back-up site upon network partition. This is because in the personal computer environment which we are considering, a typical reason for a file not being available is that its owner is running his machine stand-alone, for example at home where he has no high bandwidth access to the network. Hence a master file is quite likely to be modified by its owner whilst inaccessible to other users. Inhibiting modifications by other users in this situation avoids any problem in reconciling different versions of the same logical file: the master copy always prevails. The "multiple copy update" problem[43] is thus avoided rather than solved. Note that any system which attempts to allow "multiple copy updates" can only reconcile independent modifications to the same file if it has some knowledge of the semantics of the file contents.

Our scheme can lead to a situation where a user cannot perform some action due to the unavailability of a master file which he wishes to modify. However, since a user typically has master copies of his files on his own machine, he is not normally inhibited when running stand-alone. Obviously this does not help when several co-operating users need to modify the same files. Their problem may be reduced by locating the shared files on a "server" machine. Should this machine become unavailable due to network or machine failure then there is still the possibility of moving its disks to another machine. If, despite these measures, there is still a need to modify a file when the master is unavailable (for example the disk itself may not be operational or it may be impractical to take the measures mentioned above), then the file system clearly offers no direct help. In this situation a new (logical) file must be created and copied to the original when the latter becomes available. Any resultant mutual inconsistency must then be handled either informally or by higher level software.

3.3.2 File System Object Naming

The heart of the file system architecture is its low-level naming scheme. It is based on that used in UNIX, but extended to take account of distribution and replication. No attempt has been made to maintain compatibility with existing UNIX systems, thus freeing us from some of the problems faced by a system such as LOCUS[84] which attempts to be application code compatible with UNIX.

A PULSE distributed filestore consists of a set of "logical files" numbered 1 to n (where n is currently represented within 32 bits). This number is termed the file's file identifier, or i-number, and identifies the logical file uniquely at a given time. Once a file has been deleted its i-number may be reallocated to a new file. To preserve uniqueness in both time and space, a number (currently 16 bits long) termed an "i-sequence number" is combined with an i-number to give a file's "global i-number".

"File copies" are stored on a number of disk volumes, which are of two types, master and duplicate. Each such volume occupies part of one or more physical disks connected to a single machine. Each volume is restricted to holding copies of files whose i-numbers lie within a contiguous range. This range, along with an indication of the volume's type, are included in each volume's "volume identifier", which is stored in the volume itself. The naming scheme attempts to minimise the amount of work which must be performed by a file server to check whether its machine has a copy of a file with a given global i-number.

3.3.2.1 Master Volumes

Master volumes contain the primary, modifiable file copies. Each master file is represented by an i-node which contains the file's attributes (such as file type, owner, reference count etc.), a version number (which is incremented upon file update), and addresses of the file's data blocks (termed its disk address map). Each i-node also contains an indication of whether it is currently allocated to a file, and its i-sequence number, which is incremented whenever the i-node is applied to a new file.

3.3.2.2 Duplicate Volumes

Duplicate volumes contain the subsidiary, read-only copies of files. Each duplicate file is represented by a "duplicate i-node" which is the same, in most respects, as that of the corresponding master. The major difference is the disk address map of the file's data, which refers to the duplicate volume itself rather than the master. A further difference is the "duplication mode" which indicates, for a duplicate directory only, whether new files created within the master directory are to be automatically duplicated. The duplication mode has an initial value derived from its corresponding master, but unlike other attributes may be changed independently. No information concerning any duplicate files is kept in the master file's i-node. This facilitates the creation and deletion of duplicate copies when the master is unavailable.

3.3.2.3 I-number Allocation

Each volume, when created, is assigned a contiguous range of i-numbers, the maximum size of which is currently represented within 16 bits. Each master volume is assigned a non-overlapping range, whose associated i-node space is allocated in contiguous disk blocks. Each i-number is hence associated with a single master volume. The disk address of its corresponding master i-node may be computed directly from itself and its associated master volume's identifier. We expect many master volumes to exist (at least one for each user), but the size of individual ranges to be typically low, for example a few thousand.

Duplicate volumes, on the other hand, are assigned ranges which may overlap with each other. In order that one duplicate volume may duplicate files from many master volumes we must assign it a relatively large range of i-numbers. It is not, however, practical to allocate space statically for all potential i-node copies. To overcome this problem, each duplicate volume has a table, termed its i-map, which gives a mapping from i-number to local i-node address. The i-map has an entry for every i-number in the range assigned to the volume, a null entry indicating that the file is not duplicated. We may thus allocate as little i-node space as we expect to need, and avoid allocating i-node space for every file not currently duplicated. The storage overhead of an unduplicated file is reduced from the i-node size itself, currently 64 bytes, to 2 bytes. For a maximum size duplicate volume (in terms of number of potential files), this overhead is 256 disk blocks (each 512 bytes long), about 1 per cent of a ten megabyte disk. Without the i-map, 8092 blocks, or about 40 per cent, of a 10 megabyte disk would need to be allocated for i-node space. The introduction of the i-map does introduce an extra disk access when first referencing a duplicate file, however this is often eliminated by the file server's disk cache.

3.3.2.4 Directories

A directory is a structured file, each entry of which indicates a mapping from a textual pathname component to a global i-number. When using a directory entry to resolve a pathname string, the file server always checks the global i-number of the located i-node, and rejects it if it does not match. A new file is always allocated an i-node which resides on the same master volume as its parent directory. This scheme enables i-numbers, and hence i-nodes, to be re-used independently of other volumes. If any other volume contains a directory with a reference to the same (reallocated) i-number then no confusion arises.

The whole "logical" filestore is constrained to represent a single tree, the root of which has a well known global i-number. UNIX-style "links" provide exceptions to this rule; links across master volume boundaries are allowed but not included in a file's reference count.

3.3.3 File Location

PULSE disk volumes are not permanently bound to particular physical devices. Apart from varying availability at a single site, their location may vary due to the physical movement of removable disks and even disk units themselves. Whenever a non-local file is to be referenced we are therefore faced with the problem of finding a machine with an appropriate volume on-line. In particular we wish to achieve this with a minimum disruption to service in the face of individual disk volumes and complete machines joining and leaving the network. Ideally each machine connected to the network should always know exactly which volumes are on-line at all other sites. In a dynamic situation, where volumes are not bound to any particular site, it is inevitable that some form of broadcasting must be employed. Simply broadcasting changes in state is not sufficient, for a machine joining the network must obtain the current global state to make any sense of such information. An alternative, used in PULSE, is to find the location of a remote volume on demand.

Each file server maintains a list of locally on-line volumes. When it desires access to a remote file it broadcasts a request, quoting the file's global i-number and whether a master or duplicate copy is required. This is straightforward when a master copy of a file is to be accessed since only one volume can satisfy the request. Once its location has been found then further references to files on the same volume may be made directly without repeating the broadcast. However, if a duplicate file is to be accessed remotely, there may be several volumes containing a copy.

One method is to broadcast a request for a copy of a particular file and wait for a certain length of time; each machine having a copy replies and the most up-to-date is used. Such a scheme, however, imposes significant overhead in locating a duplicate file, both for the requester and the sites holding copies. A simpler scheme, adopted in PULSE, is to enlist the user's help and let him indicate which remote duplicate volumes are to be considered. Although reducing overall transparency, this method speeds access and is probably sufficient for most purposes. The user may be helped by the provision of a replicated file indicating mappings from user-oriented duplicate volume names to volume identifiers.

The technique of looking for volumes on demand, combined with the existence of permanent cross-volume references within directories, enables the global tree to be traversed without the need for a replicated network-wide "mount table" such as that required in LOCUS[103].

3.3.4 Duplicate File Synchronisation

Updating a duplicate file to reflect the contents of its corresponding master is termed "duplicate file synchronisation". A policy of synchronise-on-reference is currently pursued. No attempt is made, unlike LOCUS[84], to update duplicate copies of a file as soon as the master copy has been modified. Instead we take into account the expected pattern of file access in a personal computer environment whose typical usage is program development. This pattern is one of frequent modifications to local master files whose duplicate "back-up" copies are occasionally synchronised, and infrequent modifications to widely replicated files such as utility programs and system documentation. Synchronisation-upon-reference avoids needless propagation of changes to files, allowing the user to control the time of synchronisation, yet still allows a consistent view of the distributed file system to be maintained.

A utility may use the synchronise-on-reference facility to ensure a complete duplicate volume is up to date. Such a utility might be run on a user's own machine before and after running stand-alone. To force synchronisation of a remote duplicate volume a request must be sent to provoke its execution at the remote site. Clearly if a machine crashes or is withdrawn from the network without running the synchronisation utility then it may have out-of-date copies of some duplicate files. We argue that the simplicity of the synchronisation-on-reference scheme outweighs this disadvantage.

Synchronisation-on-reference is performed, at a user's discretion, when any attempt is made to access a local duplicate file for reading only. For example when opening it for reading, when inquiring about its attributes, or during a pathname search. The local file server checks to see if the master copy is available, by communicating with remote file servers when necessary, and if so, compares version numbers stored in the two i-nodes. If the duplicate file has a lower version number, then it is out-of-date and is immediately updated from the master copy. The use of version numbers instead of "time stamps" avoids the need for a global concept of time, which is difficult to provide in a distributed system[62]. The updating of the duplicate file is treated as an atomic transaction[64] to avoid the possibility of an internally inconsistent copy being created. This is achieved trivially by manipulating the i-map mentioned is section 3.2.2.3. Whilst the new copy is being created the old one may still be opened; its data will only be deleted after the last close. An attempt to synchronise with a master file which is itself currently being modified is rejected.

3.3.5 File Protection

The file protection scheme provided by the PULSE distributed file system is based on that of UNIX. User identifiers are global, and a replicated password file contains the mappings from user names to user identifiers. Protection is defensive rather than absolute, in that it relies on each machine running only PULSE software; no protection is afforded against the malicious user. A more sophisticated mechanism, such as that suggested by Gifford[34], would be needed in a "hostile" environment.

3.4 User Control

Although the file system may be used without regard for the location of files, the user may exert explicit control when necessary. He may influence which file copies are chosen to represent the logical files he wishes to access and explicitly control the amount of file replication performed on his machine.

3.4.1 File Selection Control

When a user references a file he may be considered to be using one of four file classes. These are

1)   local master,

2)   local duplicate,

3)   remote master and

4)   remote duplicate.

In response to a client's request to access a file, the file server attempts to find a copy in the order given. The user may, however, override this default behaviour. For each of its clients the file server maintains an attribute, called the "file map", which specifies the classes of file which the client wishes to be considered for selection, and the order in which their access such be attempted. A further attribute indicates whether synchronisation-on-reference is to be performed, subject to both master and duplicate file access also being requested. These attributes are adjustable by the client and inherited by further programs it may invoke. The file server always takes account of whether the access is for modification, in which case no duplicate class is considered. In particular, file creation and deletion imply the modification of that file's parent directory.

The PULSE command interpreter provides the command "setmap" to inspect and alter its own file selection control attributes. The user is thus given the ability to control the extent of remote file access performed on his behalf. A further file server facility enables him to exercise complete control over his machine: he may at any time revoke the right of others to access files, regardless of normal file protection. It is presumed that normal social pressures and the ethics of co-operation will restrict the activities of parasitic users.

3.4.2 File Replication Control

We have mentioned that a duplicate file may not be modified directly, and is changed only in the course of making it up-to-date with its master. Special cases of this are embodied in privileged programs which may be used to manipulate duplicate volumes explicitly, and may be invoked whilst running stand-alone or connected to the network.

One utility creates a duplicate copy of a master file, and another enables duplicate files to be deleted. Directories pose a special problem, in that should a duplicate file's parent directory become unavailable, the files accessed through it will effectively disappear from the user's view. This is prevented from happening by enforcing the rules that a file may only be duplicated if its parent directory is already duplicated, and that a duplicate directory may only be deleted when all duplicate files within it have themselves been deleted. Options are provided to override these restrictions. Finally there is a utility which alters the duplication mode of a duplicate directory. When set this mode causes sub-trees of the global file hierarchy to be duplicated automatically during synchronisation.

These simple programs allow a user to tailor a duplicate volume to his precise requirements, taking into account its storage capacity.

3.5 The File Server as a Distributed Name Server

If user programs are to use the IPC facilities to communicate directly, some means is needed to establish communication paths between them. The file server therefore provides a service which enables a client to associate dynamically an arbitrary Medium with a file name in the global hierarchy. This file name may then be presented to a file server by another program and a capability to the Medium granted, subject to conventional file protection. A similar mechanism is provided in the IPC extension to UNIX, developed at Carnegie-Mellon University[88]. By applying this concept within an integrated distributed file system which replicates directories, the PULSE file system acts as a distributed name server. It assists the setting up of arbitrary communication paths between programs which may be running on different machines. In particular, these paths may be used by users to provide services to others, and in general, to assist programs which themselves are distributed. The location of any such service is independent of the pathname that accesses it. It follows that the failure of a server on one machine can be remedied by the initiation of another elsewhere, without needing a different set of client programs.

3.6 File Server Communication Protocols

Communication with the file server is solely through Mediums. Each client has a capability to a distinct Medium owned by the file server, and is granted access to a further Medium whenever it successfully opens a file, through which requests pertaining to the open file may be sent. Even if a file is remote, requests are still directed to a Medium owned by the local file server. File servers communicate, using a "private" interface at a level similar to that of the Cambridge File Server[25], to perform remote file access on behalf of a client. This enables remote file operations to be implemented between file servers as repeatable transactions. State information, such as current position in the file, is held locally, and requests to read and write include the offset in the file at which to start. The advantages of such an approach are outlined by Mitchell and Dion[78]. In particular, it enables PULSE file servers to communicate without relying upon any guarantee of message delivery from the IPC service, yet requires only a simple protocol to be agreed between them.

Directing remote file requests via the local file server, unlike the Spice file system[102] which returns the user an IPC channel to the remote file server itself, thus results in two major benefits. Firstly, failure of a remote machine results in an Ada exception being raised in the local file server, rather than the user program. Currently this generates an error report, but could, for instance, initiate an attempt to find a copy of the file elsewhere. Secondly, a typical read or write to a remote file results in just two low-level data packets being sent between machines, the request and its reply.

At present the use of Mediums for non-repeatable transactions does not extend reliably across machine boundaries, unless the user imposes his own more complex protocol. Such a "reliable Medium" protocol is best implemented by the underlying IPC support, and will inevitably involve more message traffic between machines.

3.7 Summary

An integrated distributed file system for a network of personal computers has been designed and implemented. Simple mechanisms have been used to provide a natural extension to a traditional time-sharing environment for the personal computer user. We have made a particular effort to allow the user to control the work done on his behalf, whilst maintaining suitable defaults for the naive user. The simplifications we have made, compared to systems such as Spice[102] and LOCUS[84], are reflected in a lack of certain features which may be desirable in a more general purpose environment, but have contributed to a simplicity of design and implementation. In particular, in the absence of heavy usage, we cannot comment upon any practical disadvantages arising from the inability to perform multiple copy updates. However, we have found that there are situations in which a simple primary copy strategy is sufficient.

Finally, we have found that the integration of the naming of IPC channels into the distributed file system, thereby giving a consistent network transparent access mechanism to all resources, is a powerful feature upon which to build higher level distributed software.

4 THE PULSE USER INTERFACE

4.1 Introduction

An early goal of the PULSE design was that it should present functional behaviour and a user interface very similar to that of the UNIX operating system. In this chapter we discuss the facilities provided by the PULSE operating system and compare them with those found in UNIX. We then examine how we have provided a UNIX-like command interface or "Shell"[13] in terms of "UNIX-unlike" system primitives.

Although PULSE is a distributed system we have aimed to make distribution transparent to the user: it is not normally visible at command level, and will not feature much in this chapter.

Because PULSE supports Ada, programs on it may express parallel activity purely in linguistic terms. As well as this, we have seen that PULSE offers rather more general mechanisms for communication than does UNIX. We feel that the combination of these two features can make the resolution of certain problems more understandable. The design and implementation of a reasonably complex program, in this case a command language interpreter, will present an opportunity to test this claim.

4.2 UNIX System Facilities

On UNIX, user action is expressed in terms of the file system. This is controlled by a portion of the kernel, which as a whole is responsible for the management of the system. User programs are given a set of system calls as the sole interface to the kernel. Because control of the file system and general management are tightly linked, their interactions are efficient, but at a cost of limiting flexibility. For example, it is not possible to change file system behaviour without re-engineering the kernel as a whole.

UNIX provides the following basic operations and facilities.

Operating Context

Each running program can assume that a certain context is implicitly established for it. This contains such information as the user and group identifiers, the current working directory, and files opened by the program which performed the invocation, and simultaneously shared with it. This implicit sharing of already open files is an important part of the behaviour of UNIX, and pervades other mechanisms. The context also includes the process identifier of the current program and that of its invoker, or parent. This relationship allows a parent to monitor the progress of its children, and allows limited communication from the children to their parent.

Each user program has access to a library of system call routines, which function within the operating context. The following are the most relevant to our discussion.

File Control

There are calls to open, close, read and write files. Files are accessed through descriptors, which have to be identified for each operation after opening. A request peculiar to UNIX is "duplicate" or "dup". It allows a program to be allocated a new file descriptor which accesses the same open file as an existing descriptor; because descriptors are allocated on a "first-free" principle, the mechanism allows arbitrarily opened files to be accessed through known descriptors.

Fork

This expresses both parallel activity and the creation of new programs. Its effect is to spawn a new running program which is an exact textual copy of the caller of "fork". Everything is inherited from the parent except the process identifiers. However, the new program is in a different address space from its parent, and its subsequent behaviour cannot affect any of the parent's data.

Normally, after a fork call, a program must examine the returned value to determine whether it is the parent or child. This will be seen in the examples given later.

Exec

This allows a program to overwrite its code and data with the contents of a named (executable) file, and pass a set of text strings (usually as program parameters) to the resulting new image. The only possible change an "exec" call can make to the operating context is the alteration of the effective user or group identification: this allows a new program to run with different privileges from its parent, and is called the "setuid" facility[92]. Other environmental changes must be made by the programs after they start running.

Exit

This combines the duties of terminating a program and of passing a numeric value back to its invoker. The user-supplied value is combined with one supplied by the kernel, and is used as described under "Wait" below. Should no call of "exit" be made, a zero value is passed to the invoking program.

Wait

A parent can issue a call to await the termination of any of its immediate children. When the call returns, the process identifier of the terminating child and its numeric exit status are made available. Because of this information, a program can control its own behaviour according to the state of its children; the exit status conventionally has zero value for successful termination, and non-zero otherwise.

4.3 PULSE System Facilities

Like UNIX, the PULSE user expresses most action in terms of a file system. Unlike UNIX, PULSE separates file system control from the kernel. This has resulted in some loss of efficiency, but flexibility and modularity are increased: for example, a new file system could be developed and used concurrently with the original, and without affecting existing users. The file system is controlled by a multi-task Ada program which communicates with the kernel and with user programs by means of the PULSE IPC. The IPC is the only means of access to system facilities. For everyday use, the calls are encapsulated in Ada packages which provide a UNIX-like procedural interface to user programs (see chapter 5 and appendix B).

The most striking difference from UNIX is the absence of a "fork" request; this decision about the design was made for the following reasons. To duplicate the image of a single thread of control is reasonable: it can be guaranteed that the only pending system call is the fork itself, and that no other conflict can arise. On the other hand, where there are several concurrent threads of control, each potentially making system requests, the concept of process duplication becomes difficult. If one task makes the request, what is to become of the others? Should they be aborted? If they are, what becomes of the program as a whole?

PULSE therefore separates the concerns of parallel activity and program creation. The Ada language, which PULSE supports, defines its own model of parallel activity (tasking), and the means by which tasks may communicate. Since we have suggested that the fork is unsuitable in this situation we provide a different mechanism for program creation, which is described below.

4.3.1 PULSE Kernel

The facilities of the kernel are these.

Run-time Support for Ada

Support is given for tasking and exceptions. Each task within a program is scheduled individually: should one task be blocked, others may continue to do useful work.

IPC

This is expressed as entry calls to tasks in the kernel (Mediums). Medium capabilities may be created by the kernel or may be passed or copied from one program to another. Unlike UNIX open files, this transfer must be explicit: there is no implicit inheritance.

If a program tries to access a Medium for which there is no reader, no writer, or for which it has no capability, exceptions are raised in the task which makes the relevant entry call.

Program Execution

A PULSE program can request the ability to load a stream of bytes and start it running. By convention it is the file system which does this on behalf of user programs.

Network Server

The PULSE IPC is extended to other machines by a network server, which also monitors the state of remote systems, and is responsible for the raising of the appropriate exceptions in those programs which use it. The network server also provides a broadcast service whereby local messages received on its "broadcast Medium" will be sent to all other network servers via their "global Medium". A program may receive such "broadcast" messages by requesting its local network server to forward messages received on its "global Medium". In practice only the file servers use these broadcast facilities.

Like the file server, the network server can run as a program separate from the kernel; in the prototype system, however, it is implemented as a part of the kernel.

Access to Local Devices

Local devices may be accessed via the IPC through Mediums owned by the kernel.

4.3.2 File Server Operations

The file system defines a set of operations which are implemented using the kernel facilities.

File Server Request Medium

In order to use the file server at all, a user program must have access to a Medium through which requests are made. Each program invoked through the file server is allocated its own such Medium and is given a capability for it when it starts running. Moreover, like other capabilities, it may be passed from one program to another.

File System Context

This defines the expected context in which a given Request Medium is used. Like UNIX it defines the current directory, the user and group identifiers, and the program identifier of the current and parent programs. It can also determine the behaviour of the file system in relation to the network. The file system maintains a UNIX-like parent-child relationship between programs. No IPC capabilities are inherited from the parent.

Various requests may be made of the file system, of which the following are the most pertinent.

File Control

The standard requests to open, read, and write files are all available. The open request is directed along the Request Medium, and returns with a new IPC capability which is used for subsequent operations on the open file. Files are closed simply by relinquishing the capability. Like UNIX, many programs can access the same open file, except that the effect is achieved by the explicit sharing of capabilities rather than the implicit inheritance of file descriptors.

Clone

This gives a program a new file system context, and a Medium with which to access it. For the purposes of discussion, we will term such contexts as "secondary": the "primary" context is that which a program has when it starts. The ability to access several contexts allows a program to do similar actions in different environments - for example two tasks could work with two contexts which have different working directories.

Exec

This is a file system request which may only be directed along a Medium belonging to a secondary context. It causes a named program to be loaded and started. The Medium capability used for the "exec" is transferred to the new program, and revoked from the caller; the context becomes the primary context for the child. This prevents the parent from gaining "setuid"-like privileges gained as a result of the "exec".

Set Exit Status

Unlike UNIX, PULSE separates the concerns of program termination and of setting the exit status. As was the case with "fork", it is not apparent how a multi-task program should behave if a termination request is made by a subsidiary task. We therefore limit the control of termination to the notification of the intended exit value: no explicit notification results in a value of zero. Programs terminate as the result of normal completion: there is no extra mechanism.

Wait/Nowait

This is issued along the request Medium for a program's primary context, and allows a parent to await or disown a named child. On return, wait gives its caller the exit status of the child; nowait does not. The exit status may be used in similar fashion to UNIX. A terminated child will remain dormant until a parent makes a wait or nowait request. A nowait request returns immediately and allows a child program to proceed and terminate without regard for the parent.

4.4 The Command Language

The traditional role of a command language is to enable a user to invoke programs, and to control how they are invoked. On some systems there is a clear separation between facilities available to programs and those available at command level. Commands may be interpreted by a portion of the operating system executive which is accessible by users. More recent usage, however, has tended to make all system facilities pertinent to commands and program invocation available to programming languages. Indeed, on PULSE and UNIX, the only access to system facilities is in this way: a command language on these systems is implemented by a separate program. Such a program needs no special privileges, because the relevant system primitives are freely available to all programs. We are examining, therefore, the user program which implements the command language on PULSE, and comparing it with the corresponding program on UNIX.

4.4.1 User Interaction

Users develop a mental model of system behaviour as the result of using a command language[69,35]. They perceive the behaviour of the system as indivisible from the structure and semantics of the language. In trying to give one system a command language with the meaning and structure derived from another, we are effectively trying to move a model of system behaviour.

There are several ways of moving such a model. Perhaps the most obvious method is to move the language and its interpreter unchanged: this will require the provision of sufficient support to allow it to run. Most comprehensive would be to move the operating system as a whole. However, this may not always be the most suitable or advisable course. It may be better to identify the characterising features of the original model, and implement a new language which embodies them. Once the language and its behaviour is defined, we must then identify the characteristics of the underlying system which will allow that language to be realised.

Our approach is as follows. First we discuss the structure and facilities of the shell independently of the two systems. Because the "model" language was developed entirely in terms of UNIX, it seems appropriate to discuss briefly how it works on it. Only then will we discuss its implementation on PULSE.

4.5 The UNIX and PULSE Command Interface

The language implemented as the PULSE Shell is a subset of the UNIX "Bourne" Shell[13]. In general terms, a command is expressed as

      command_name arg1 arg2 ... argn

We will not consider further the lexical representation of this: we are more concerned here with the mapping of shell semantics on to the underlying system. Nevertheless, the syntactic representation of programs as commands plays a significant role in the development of the user's perceived model of system behaviour. In particular it allows the user to add to or even replace existing members of the repertoire of commands, enabling personal tailoring of a particular working environment.

A command may be a program or an internal shell operation. The shell operations change the environment for the current shell, and for commands subsequently executed by it: for example, one changes the current directory. Similarly arguments may be passed as strings to the appropriate program, or may be instructions to the shell about how a program is to be invoked. The shell arguments concern the association of "standard" input/output streams with named files: this is another contributor to the user's model of system behaviour - he does not have to write special versions of programs depending on the source or destination of input and output.

Besides its basic command structure, the shell language common to UNIX and PULSE has constructs for program composition using "pipes", for background (or parallel) invocation, and for simple conditional invocation. Background invocation implies that once the command is accepted, the shell returns immediately to the user for more input, and the original command is evaluated in parallel.

Let us summarise the main components of interaction using the shell.

1) Any action, be it program invocation or environmental control, is expressed as a command.

2) The command repertoire is extensible, and the use of added commands is transparent to the user.

3) Input output requirements of programs can be finalised at invocation time.

4) Programs can be interconnected using pipes.

5) The issuing of a command can be made dependent on the outcome of a previous one.

6) A command can be issued in such a way as to be processed in parallel to the issuing and processing of other commands.

Disregarding the fact that the shell was developed originally for and on UNIX, let us consider the requirements of the various constructs.

1) There is some implicit parallelism in the ability to invoke a program and then to return for more input. This is made more clear by the ability to invoke programs in the background. To implement a straightforward scheme suggests that one program should be able to invoke another without itself being destroyed in the process.

2) There should be some system-wide convention of passing arguments from one program to another. This may be achieved in different ways: text may be copied into the new program's address space, or information may be passed explicitly between running programs or in files. The only requirement is that there is an agreed protocol.

3) There must be a way to provide initial values for input and output channels. As with arguments, this may be in terms of information passed at invocation time, or it may be in terms of an agreed protocol after the new program has started.

4) There is some information passed back from the new program to the old after the new program has terminated. This is so that conditional invocation may be implemented.

Passing of arguments and the return of an exit status places no peculiar demands on a system: it merely requires that suitable protocols be devised. The major constraints on a command language processor are therefore the ability first to retain execution context between commands, second, to express parallel activity, and third, to set up the sharing of I/O channels between programs. We will now examine UNIX and PULSE in the light of these requirements, after touching briefly on behaviour common to both systems.

4.5.1 Initial Behaviour

Both the PULSE and UNIX shells behave similarly in their treatment of the user's input. The command line is analysed and a syntax tree produced, non-terminal nodes of which determine the combination and control of commands, that is in respect of pipelines, conditionals, sequences and background invocation, and terminal nodes of which are the commands themselves. The terminal nodes also carry parameter lists and file-oriented i/o redirections. By traversing the tree, the shell causes programs to be invoked in the proper order and with the appropriate parallelism.

We will now consider the interactions between system and shell program, for UNIX and PULSE.

4.5.2 UNIX Expression of Shell Commands

For the simplest commands which invoke programs the basic behaviour is shown in Figure 4.1: the shell program forks, and the child then issues an "exec" call with the appropriate arguments. (Exec has two common expressions: execv, where a vector of arguments is given, and execl, where a list is given.)

```
run_program( progfile, progname, arg1, ... , argn, 0)
char *progfile, *progname, *arg1,...,*argn;
{
    int pid, exit_val;

    pid = fork();
    if(pid == -1){
        /* fork failed */
    } else if(pid == 0){
        /* child process */
        execl( progfile, progname, arg1, arg2,..., argn, 0);
        /* return here indicates exec failed */
    } else {
        /* parent */
        if(foreground){
            pid = wait(&exit_val);
        }
    }
}
```

Figure 4.1: Program Invocation in UNIX

Manipulation of the new environment usually takes place between the "fork" and "exec". The following example, Figure 4.2, shows the most common case of this where existing input/output streams are to be associated with named files. Because the child program has inherited the parent's standard streams, it is necessary to close them before opening them for the new access.

```
run_prog(progfile, progname, arg1, ....)
char *progfile, *progname, *arg1;
{
    int pid, exit_val;
    pid = fork();
    if(pid == -1){
        /* fork failed */
    } else if(pid == 0){
        /* child process */
        close(STD_INPUT);
        if(fd = open(newifile, 0)) != STD_INPUT){
                /* open failed */ ;
        }
        close(STD_OUTPUT);
        if((fd = open(newofile, 2)) != STD_OUTPUT){
                /* open failed */ ;
        }
        /* new program retains these files */
        execl(progfile, progname, arg1, arg2,..., argn, 0);
        /* return here indicates exec failed */
    } else {
        /* parent: still has old open files */
        if(foreground){
            pid = wait(&exit_val);
        }
    }
}
```

Figure 4.2: Manipulation of the Environment in UNIX

A pipe requires the invocation of two programs, with the proper connections made between them, see Figure 4.3. As with simple redirection, each program must close those inherited channels it intends to change. Other manipulations are not shown in the example.

```
run_program(prog1file, prog2file, ...)
char *prog1file, *prog2file,...;
{
    int pid_send, pid_recv, exit_val;
    int pv[2];

    pipe(pv);          /* set up pipe file descriptors
                        * pv[0] input end
                        * pv[1] output end */
    pid_recv = fork();
    if(pid_recv == -1){
        /* fork failed */
    } else if(pid_recv == 0){
        /* receiving child process */
        close(STD_INPUT);
        close(pv[1]); /* close this copy of the output
                       * end of the pipe */
        dup(pv[0]); /* grab a synonymous file desc as
                     * pipe input should be STD_INPUT */
        /* new program retains these files */
        execl(prog1file, prog1name, arg1, ..., argn, 0);
        /* return here indicates exec failed */
    } else {
        /* parent */
        /* still has old open files */
        pid_send = fork();
        if(pid_send == 0) {
            /* sending child process */
            close(pv[0]); /* close input end of pipe */
            close(STD_OUTPUT);
            dup(pv[1]); /* as above, but for output end */
            execl(prog2file, prog2name, arg1, 0);
            /* return here is failed exec */
        } else {
            /* parent */
            if(foreground){
                es = wait(&exit_val);
            }
        }
    }
}
```

Figure 4.3: Setting up a UNIX Pipe

Conditional invocation simply requires that the shell program examines the exit status of a child before deciding which program to invoke next. In all the above fragments, the parent checks whether the invocation is "foreground" or "background": foreground activity requires the parent to wait while background does not. In fact the UNIX shell always forks for background work, with the effect that internal commands invoked in the background have no effect on the current shell.

A useful facility is the parenthesising of commands: these are run in a "subshell", with all shell operations applying to the subshell as a whole. Because the fork creates an identical running image of a program, subshells are trivially implemented on UNIX, since the new program inherits the data structures describing the parenthesised command.

The implicit parallelism required for program invocation is provided by the use of "fork". Once the parallel process is established, the use of "exec" starts the new named program. Without "fork", the only method of program invocation would be destructive. Arguments are built into "exec": they are retained in the address space across the call. Initial input/output channels are passed by inheritance, rather than by explicit action. The result is that changing them requires their closure and re-opening. Finally, termination values are built into the invocation scheme, and are simply accessed by system call.

Although the "fork" does not appear, at least at first sight, to be the most obvious method of achieving the requirements for a shell language, it does encapsulate all the necessary actions for setting up and controlling the environment for a new program. In particular it provides a mechanism for the sharing of I/O channels.

4.5.3 PULSE Expression of Shell Commands

In PULSE, we are attempting to map a model of user interaction developed on UNIX onto a system which offers rather different facilities. The most significant problem is that of the different expression of parallel activity and program creation. Unlike UNIX, program invocation does not require any expression of parallel activity by the invoker. For pipelines and background invocations, however, explicit parallelism is required: this requires the use of Ada tasks within the shell program itself. Thus, whenever two programs are invoked to run concurrently, the subtree which contains the relevant command sequence is passed to a task and the traversal continues in parallel with traversal of other (higher) subtrees. Once a subtree has been passed for concurrent traversal, there is no further interaction with the main task. It is this explicit use and expression of parallelism in the program itself which we felt would aid the understanding of the design. However, because the same routine is used for tree traversal whether or not it is called from the main task or from a subsidiary one, the actual visible use of parallel activity is slight, and is really no more than in UNIX. The following example, Figure 4.4, should give some feel of what is involved in traversing the tree. Reference is made in it to routines and entries which are defined in subsequent examples.

```
procedure tree_walk(tree: shell_tree_t) is

   -- a skeleton procedure for evaluating a shell parse
   -- tree; many declarations and details are omitted

begin
    case tree.node_type is
        when PROGRAM =>
            -- leaf node
            run_program(tree.prog_name,...);
        when PIPE =>
            -- adds pipe info to program info
            set_pipe(tree);
            controller.get_worker(tree.left,...);
            -- evaluation goes on in parallel
            tree_walk(tree.right,...);
        when BACKGROUND =>
            controller.get_worker(tree.left,...);
            -- other operations
    end case;
end tree_walk;
```

Figure 4.4: Evaluation of the PULSE Shell's Parse Tree

Basic invocation (for terminal nodes) proceeds as follows. The shell program issues a clone request, then issues an execute request down the new Medium. It then explicitly passes arguments along a "lifeline" Medium. These consist of the standard i/o Mediums, and any textual arguments that may be necessary. By convention, the default i/o capabilities are those with which the shell program itself was passed. Figure 4.5 shows the necessary Ada code, it assumes much in the way of declarations and is given only to give some flavour of the sequence of actions. **Lifeline** is the channel between the parent and the child programs, and the parameter **to_wait** indicates whether the routine is to wait for the child to terminate.

```
procedure run_program(prog_name: name_t,
                      to_wait: boolean,...) is
begin
    clone(lifeline, r_pid); -- set up secondary context
    exec(prog_name, lifeline, priority);
    -- the protocol for arguments is to send
    -- an initial null message with counts
    -- of IPC and text arguments
    nulmsg.user_code := strcount;  -- text count
    nulmsg.my_ref := medcount;     -- IPC count
    lifeline.send_message(nulmsg); -- send them
    -- m_vec contains a list of IPC arguments
    -- send them
    for i in m_vec'first .. m_vec'last loop
        nulmsg.reply := m_vec(i);
        lifeline.send_message(nulmsg);
    end loop;
    -- always send at least one text
    -- argument: program name
    unsdata.adr := s_vec.name.txt'address;
    unsdata.count := s_vec.name.count;
    lifeline.send_message(unsafemsg);
    str_p := s_vec.arg_head;
    -- send remaining text arguments
    while str_p /= null loop
        unsdata.adr := str_p.text.txt'address;
        unsdata.count := str_p.text.count;
        lifeline.send_message(unsafemsg);
        str_p := str_p.right;
    end loop;

    -- wait is not depending on requirements
    if to_wait then
        exit_status := wait(req_med);
    else
        exit_status := nowait(req_med);
    end if;
exception
    when NO_READER | NO_WRITER =>
        -- clean up
end run_program;
```

Figure 4.5: PULSE Program Invocation and Parameter Passing

PULSE Shell Implementation   61

Unlike UNIX, files do not have to be closed if there is explicit redirection of I/O: in any case, all IPC channels must be passed explicitly irrespective of any other control. If there is explicit redirection, then the appropriate file is simply opened before "run_program" is called and the resulting capabilities added to the traversal information for the appropriate tree node.

A pipeline is expressed as a non-terminal node whose left subtree is passed to a task, and whose right subtree is traversed directly. Before starting the parallel traversal the pipe is set up and as with redirected I/O, added to the traversal information for each subtree.

Conditional invocation uses the exit status available after the return of a "wait" request. There is no real difference from UNIX.

As with pipes, background invocation requires that the relevant subtree be passed to a task. In this case, the shell issues a "nowait" request so that work may continue.

Unlike UNIX, subshells are not easy to implement. The relevant sequence of commands must be collected as input to an explicit invocation of the shell program, with all the requisite IPC control. As yet, this has not been implemented.

4.6 Discussion of PULSE Shell Implementation

The most significant features in the PULSE shell are the use of Ada tasks to express parallel invocation, and the passing of arguments after the new program has started.

4.6.1 Tasking

The use of tasks is found in much of PULSE, and has consequences not restricted to the shell. Ada offers a mechanism for the dynamic creation of tasks. This means that if no tasks are needed, no cost is incurred. However, the language rules state that if variables of a task access type are potentially visible, then some part of the created task must remain present even after the task has terminated. This has the result that if many tasks are created, and in the absence of a garbage collector (inappropriate for real-time systems, the intended subject of Ada) the program can grow beyond its address limits (see appendix C). Another point is that the PULSE kernel does not yet free all task space when it is appropriate to do so (see chapter 6).

Because of these problems, a PULSE idiom is the use of sets of statically allocated "worker" tasks, with another task to control their use (see Figure 4.6). A potential "client" needing a task, instead of using the Ada <u>new</u> operator, makes an entry on the appropriate controller, which passes the request to one of the set of workers. This proceeds smoothly until it becomes necessary that the worker tasks terminate (perhaps at "logout" time): another language rule states that a parent task cannot terminate until all child tasks have terminated. Waiting for work does not amount to termination, so the workers must be <u>aborted</u>, with possible problems of interrupting critical work, or a special request must be made to them. In the case of the shell, a null subtree is passed. If any task is still engaged in evaluating a command tree, then the parent will wait until more work is requested. The worst case occurs when argument conventions are violated, as described below. Once all the tasks have received this indication, the parent (main) task is free to terminate, possibly after notifying its caller of an exit value.

Ada does provide a superficially cleaner method of allowing tasks to terminate, by having an "or terminate" arm to a select statement. However, the construct may only be used with an "accept"-based select. Were the workers to use this facility they would not be able to queue for work in an arbitrary order: instead the controller would have to poll each task in turn using a conditional entry call. We do not consider this to be acceptable. The following example, shown in Figure 4.6, should illustrate the relevant principles. As in the previous example, much is omitted in the way of declarations.

PULSE Shell Implementation

```ada
task type worker_t;

worker : array(1..MAXWORK) of worker_t;

-- shell_tree_t is the type applicable to a shell
-- parse tree node;
-- in reality other arguments are also passed

task controller is
    entry get_worker(info: shell_tree_t);
    entry start_worker(info: out shell_tree_t);
end controller;

task body worker_t is
    this_job : shell_tree_t;
begin
    loop
        controller.start_worker(this_job);
        -- queue up for work from controller
        exit when this_job = NULL;
        -- do work by calling same routine
        -- which called for worker!
        tree_walk(this_job);

    end loop;
end worker_t;

task body controller is
begin
    accept get_worker(info: shell_tree_t) do
        accept start_worker(w_info: out shell_tree_t) do
            w_info := info;
        end start_worker;
    end get_worker;
end controller;
```

Figure 4.6: Tasking in the PULSE Shell

Work is allocated by calls like those in our first Ada example.

The use of the nested "accept" prevents clients from proceeding without allocating work, and allow clients to queue in arbitrary order. To a certain extent, this method may be counter-intuitive, in that both the sending and the receiving tasks make entry calls. Were the receiving task to have an accept, however, no arbitrary queuing would be possible.

4.6.2 Arguments

Argument passing also apparently poses a problem. It is only a PULSE convention that arguments are passed: a program can ignore them if it wishes. This means that a task in the shell could be forced to wait if a program does not read the arguments provided: it may be the main task or a worker task. At first sight, arguments could be sent using the ability to construct in a PULSE message complex combinations of data types, including the ability to transfer arbitrary lists of IPC capabilities. However, messages are of finite size, and very long lists of arguments may require several messages. Because of this, and because the prototype implementation does not yet support the transfer of lists of capabilities, the problem of blocking remains. The problem is simply solved by the behaviour of the IPC. The attempt to send messages will eventually complete after the child has terminated: the completion will be as a result of a "no_reader" exception being raised in the shell, as a defunct program loses its capabilities.

A detail description of the implementation of argument passing is given in chapter 5.

4.6.3 Performance

Because arguments are passed between running programs, and not at invocation time as in UNIX, each transaction requires a context switch, and therefore implies that PULSE must be slower than UNIX in this aspect. Moreover, in the current implementation it has the secondary effect that if the new program is large, it may be that the shell also has to be swapped out after sending each message.

4.7 Summary

We have shown that it is possible to implement a command language for PULSE which presents a model of interaction almost indistinguishable from that of UNIX. The major differences in the underlying system are firstly that UNIX binds together parallel activity and program creation, while PULSE does not, and secondly that program parameters are passed before program start in UNIX, but after it in PULSE.

The use in PULSE of language-expressed parallelism was considered initially to be an aid to construction and understanding of programs, but in the case of the shell, little real difference from UNIX has been found. Indeed in some areas, notably that of true subshells, there have been greater problems.

The use of Ada tasks has also highlighted general problems of the tasking model, in particular the constant growth in program size when tasks are created dynamically. Our solution avoids this, but at the cost of placing predefined limits on the amount of parallel activity.

5 USER PROGRAMMING

In the previous chapter we discussed the user interface to the PULSE system, and in particular its shell, or command interpreter. In this chapter we discuss, in more detail, the facilities PULSE provides for the "user level" programmer.

Several utility programs, or tools, have been developed to demonstrate PULSE's efficacy as an operating system for program development. These include an editor and other tools based on the versions found in Kernighan and Plauger[60], some UNIX-like utilities such as those concerned with directory file manipulation, and some PULSE specific utilities such as those which control file replication. Manual entries for these programs are given in appendix B. Two of these tools are used here as examples of PULSE user programs.

5.1 System Packages

The PULSE programmer has at his disposal the full Ada language augmented by several "system" packages. A short description of the major packages is now given. All the package bodies are written in Ada, although **pulse_ipc** contains some routines whose bodies are written in assembler as they contains traps into the PULSE kernel.

pstandard   Provides some standard type definitions to augment those of the Ada package standard, such as a string pointer type.

pulse_ipc   Defines the PULSE IPC. A full specification is given in appendix A.

args   Provides subprograms to access a program's arguments. It is described in detail later in this section, and a full specification is given in appendix B.

pulse_types   Defines some fundamental types and constants used by the kernel and file server, and also of occasional general use. Examples are types and constants to define a disk block sized buffer.

fs_int_types   This is the file server package which defines the types used in communicating with the file server. An example is **open_mode_t**, an object of which type must be included in an "open" or "create" message.

fs_interface   Provides a UNIX-like subprogram interface to the PULSE file server. It enables a user to ignore the actual message passing required to communicate with the file server. An open file is represented by an object of the private type **file_t**, termed its file descriptor. The implementation of an open file as a Medium capability is thus hidden. Functions are provided to enable interested programs to access the Medium associated with a file descriptor, and generate a file descriptor from a Medium. A full specification is given in appendix B.

p_text_io   This package is the PULSE programmers' alternative to Ada's standard **text_io** package. It provides buffered I/O streams, similar to that of the UNIX **stdio** package. It utilises the **fs_interface** to accomplish this, and enables many programs to avoid the direct use of the lower level package. A full specification is given in appendix B.

Any PULSE package implementation must consider the effects of it being used by more than one task in the same Ada program. **P_text_io** is a typical example whereby its private data structures must be protected from concurrent access. In fact only the allocation of buffers is protected. Two tasks performing I/O to the same buffered stream must provide their own synchronisation. Such a facility is not provided by the package itself as it would greatly degrade performance for the normal case of a single task accessing a stream.

The other packages may always be safely used by multiple tasks in the same program. In **fs_interface,** this is at the cost of allocating and deallocating message space and a reply Medium capability for each file server request. A single task program is hence less efficient than strictly necessary.

5.2 An Example Package

This section describes how parameters, or arguments, are handled in a PULSE program by presenting in detail the **args** package. It also provides an example of the use of the PULSE IPC. The full text of **args** is given in Figure 5.1.

Two types of parameters may be passed to a program: Mediums and character strings. The package provides four visible functions: two for manipulating Mediums (**argcm** and **argvm**) and two for manipulating character strings (**argc** and **argv**).

The functions argcm and argc return the number of Medium and string parameters respectively. The functions argvm and argv take an integer parameter, which indicates the number of the parameter of interest and returns the Medium and a pointer to the character string respectively. By convention the first string parameter (numbered from 0) is the name with which the program was invoked) and the first three Medium parameters (numbered from 1) refer to the program's standard input, standard output and standard error files.

Note that the package tries to avoid restrictions on the number and size of arguments, being limited only by the maximum IPC message size.

```
with pstandard, pulse_ipc, deallocation, os_interface;
use deallocation, pulse_ipc, pstandard, os_interface;

package args is
  function argc return integer;
  function argv(arg : integer) return p_string;
  function argcm return integer;
  function argvm(arg : integer) return medium;
end args;

package body args is

  lifeline : medium := constant_medium(-2);
  buffer   : p_string;
  MAX_SIZE : constant integer := 512;

  arg_mess : p_message_t;
  arg_data : p_unsafe_t;

  type med_array_t is array(natural range <>) of medium;
  type p_med_array_t is access med_array_t;
  type argc_array_t is array(natural range <>) of p_string;
  type p_argc_array_t is access argc_array_t;
  p_argc_arr : p_argc_array_t;
  p_med_arr : p_med_array_t;
  argccount, argmcount : integer;

  function argcm return integer is
  begin
    return argmcount;
  end argcm;

  function argvm(arg: integer) return medium is
  begin
    if arg < p_med_arr'first or  arg > p_med_arr'last then
      return null;
    else
      return p_med_arr(arg);
    end if;
  end argvm;

  function argc return integer is
  begin
    return argccount;
  end argc;
```

```
   function argv(arg : integer) return p_string is
   begin
     if arg < p_argc_arr'first or arg > p_argc_arr'last then
        return null;
     else
        return(p_argc_arr(arg));
     end if;
   end argv;

------------------Initialisation Code----------------------

begin
   arg_mess := new null_message_t;
   lifeline.receive_message(arg_mess);       -- get argc argcm
   argccount := arg_mess.user_code;
   argmcount := arg_mess.my_ref;
   if argmcount > 0 then
      p_med_arr := new med_array_t(1..argmcount);
      for i in 1.. argmcount loop
         arg_mess.reply := acceptreply;
         lifeline.receive_message(arg_mess);
         p_med_arr(i) := arg_mess.reply;
      end loop;
   end if;
   deallocate(arg_mess);
   if argccount > 0 then
      arg_mess := new unsafe_message_t;
      p_argc_arr := new argc_array_t(0..argccount-1);
      buffer := new string(1..MAX_SIZE);
      arg_data := new unsafe_t;
      arg_mess.dd.unsafe_data := arg_data;
      arg_data.adr := buffer.all'address;
      for i in 0 .. argccount-1 loop
         arg_data.count := MAX_SIZE;
         lifeline.receive_message(arg_mess);
         p_argc_arr(i) := new string(1..arg_data.count);
         p_argc_arr(i).all := buffer.all(1..arg_data.count);
      end loop;
      deallocate(arg_data);
      deallocate(arg_mess);
   end if;
end args;
```

Figure 5.1: The Argument Passing Package

Args exemplifies a package which must perform a fair amount of work at elaboration time: others are simpler in that they encapsulate a set of routines without needing complex initialisation.

5.3 A Simple Example Tool

In general a software tool will be constructed from a main procedure and a subset of the system packages. For example consider one of the simplest tools "echo", shown in Figure 5.2, which echos its arguments to standard output.

```
with args; with p_text_io;
with pstandard; use pstandard;
procedure main is

    argp : p_string;
begin
    for i in 1 .. args.argc-1 loop
        argp :=args.argv(i);
        p_text_io.put(argp.all);
        p_text_io.put(" ");
    end loop;
    p_text_io.new_line;
end main;
```

Figure 5.2: The Echo Tool

For its implementation the main program requires access to three packages. **Args** to get the command line arguments, **p_text_io** to do the I/O, and **p_standard** to get the type definition of a string pointer (**p_string**).

5.4 A Further Example Tool

In this section we describe a more complex tool, the PULSE "cp" utility. This program copies files in the same manner as its UNIX namesake. It is particularly interesting as it has the added capability of copying multiple files in parallel, thereby illustrating user level concurrent programming.

Further Example Tool

Several named files may be copied into a single named directory, with their original final pathname components preserved. The -p, or parallel, option causes the multiple copies to take place in parallel rather than the usual sequential order. A "worker" task being created for each file to be copied. Files may thus truly be copied in parallel, since when one task is held up waiting for I/O, the PULSE kernel may schedule another task to run.

The complete text of "cp" is presented in Figure 5.3; for convenience this program has line numbers. Compared with "echo", a further three system packages are required. **Fs_interface** and **fs_int_types** are needed to access files directly, for example to open a file to be copied (at line 60). **Pulse_types** is needed to enable a buffer to be declared (at line 50) of appropriate size, such that files may be copied a disk block at a time.

A result of 0 is returned if all files are copied successfully and 1 if any failure occurs, be it bad filenames, I/O errors etc. The main subprogram first vets the program arguments then calls function **copy** (at line 160) for each file to be copied. If the parallel option is specified then rather than call **copy** directly, "worker" tasks are created (at line 157) which themselves call **copy** (at line 115). Note the use of pragma STACK_SIZE (line 9) to limit the size of the tasks' stacks due to the address space limitations of the prototype system (see chapter 6).

The main task must rendezvous with each worker (line 158) to tell it which file to copy, since Ada has no mechanism for passing parameters to a new task. Likewise an Ada task can pass no information back upon termination. In this program the main subprogram wishes to know whether the worker tasks have succeeded in copying the files. This is achieved by the use of the shared boolean variable "result" (declared at line 10) which is set FALSE if any failure occurs. The main subprogram simply uses the Ada task termination rules to wait for the worker tasks to finish (line 165). It may then safely access the shared variable. We have thus avoided having to rendezvous with each worker to discover whether each was successful. The latter approach would have to be used if the worker tasks read the value of "result", or if updating "result" were not an indivisible operation (for example if it were a record).

Finally, we note that "cp" is a typical example of a program which ignores the existence of the network. It need concern itself neither with the distribution nor replication of files, yet may be used to copy files between machines.

```
 1  with pstandard, pulse_types, args, fs_int_types;
 2  with p_text_io, fs_interface;
 3  use pstandard, pulse_types, args, fs_int_types;
 4  use fs_interface, p_text_io;
 5
 6  procedure main is
 7   -- cp command - with parallel option
 8   -- cp file1 file2 or cp [-p] file1..filen directory2
 9   PRAGMA STACK_SIZE(1200);
10   result : integer := 0;              -- assume success
11
12   task type worker is
13    entry start_copy(source : p_string;target : p_string);
14   end;
15
16   procedure usage is
17   begin
18    put_line(stderr,"usage: cp f1 f2 or cp f1 .. f2 d2");
19   end;
20
21   function suffix(full: string) return string is
22    -- return final pathname component
23    result : p_string;
24   begin
25    for i in reverse full'first..full'last loop
26     if full(i) = '/' then
27      result := new string(1..(full'last - i));
28      result.all := full(i+1..full'last);
29      return result.all;
30     end if;
31    end loop;
32    return full;
33   end suffix;
34
35   function p_str(s : string) return p_string is
36    -- given a string, return a pointer to a copy of it
37    tmp : p_string;
38   begin
39    tmp := new string(s'first .. s'last);
40    tmp.all := s;
41    return tmp;
42   end p_str;
```

```
43  function copy(source : p_string; target : p_string)
44              return boolean is
45  -- copy file "source" to "target"
46  -- return TRUE if successful
47  real_target : p_string := target;
48  sbuf,tbuf : stat_buf_t;
49  ok : boolean;
50  iobuf : string(1 .. BLOCK_SIZE);
51  f_source, f_target : file_t;
52  n : integer;
53  mode : file_mode_t;
54  begin
55   stat(source.all, sbuf, ok);
56   if not ok then
57    put_line(stderr,"cp:cannot stat " & source.all);
58    return FALSE;
59   end if;
60   f_source := open(source.all,F_READ);
61   if f_source = NO_FILE then
62    put_line(stderr,"cp: cannot open " & source.all);
63    return FALSE;
64   end if;
65
66   mode := sbuf.mode;
67   stat(target.all, tbuf, ok);
68   if ok and then tbuf.mode.file_type = FT_DIR then
69    real_target:=p_str(target.all&"/"&suffix(source.all));
70   end if;
71   stat(real_target.all,tbuf,ok);
72
73   if ok then
74    if sbuf.global_ino = tbuf.global_ino then
75     put_line(stderr,"cp:cannot copy file to itself");
76     close(f_source);
77     return FALSE;
78    end if;
79   end if;
80   f_target := creat(real_target.all, mode);
81   if f_target = NO_FILE then
82    put_line(stderr,"cp:cannot create" & real_target.all);
83    close(f_source);
84    return FALSE;
85   end if;
```

```
 86    loop
 87      n := read(f_source, iobuf'address, BLOCK_SIZE);
 88      exit when n = 0;
 89      if n < 0 then
 91        close(f_source);
 92        close(f_target);
 93        return FALSE;
 94      end if;
 95      if write(f_target, iobuf'address, n) /= n then
 96        put_line(stderr,"cp:write error on" & real_target.all);
 97        close(f_source);
 98        close(f_target);
 99        return FALSE;
100      end if;
101    end loop;
102
103    close(f_source);
104    close(f_target);
105    return TRUE;
106  end copy;
107
108
109  task body worker is
110    s,t : p_string;
111  begin
112    accept start_copy(source : p_string;target : p_string) do
113      s := source; t := target;
114    end start_copy;
115    if not copy(s,t) then
116      result := 1;
117    end if;
118  end worker;
119
120 begin
121 declare
122   type p_worker is access worker;
123   this_worker : p_worker;
124   first_file_arg_no : integer := 1;
125   last_file_arg_no : integer := argc - 1;
126   first_arg, last_arg : p_string;
127   stat_buf : stat_buf_t;
128   popt : boolean := FALSE;
129   ok : boolean;
```

```
130 begin
131   if argc < 3 then
132     usage;
133     set_result(1);
134     return;
135   end if;
136   first_arg := argv(1);
137   if first_arg.all = "-p" then
138     popt := TRUE;
139     first_file_arg_no := 2;
140     if last_file_arg_no - first_file_arg_no < 2 then
141       usage;
142       set_result(1);
143       return;
144     end if;
145   end if;
146   if last_file_arg_no > first_file_arg_no + 1 then
147     last_arg := argv(last_file_arg_no);
148     stat(last_arg.all,stat_buf, ok);
149     if not ok or else stat_buf.mode.file_type /= FT_DIR then
150       usage;
151       set_result(1);
152       return;
153     end if;
154   end if;
155   for i in first_file_arg_no .. last_file_arg_no-1 loop
156     if popt then      -- do in parallel
157       this_worker := new worker;
158       this_worker.start_copy(argv(i),argv(last_file_arg_no));
159     else
160       if not copy(argv(i), argv(last_file_arg_no)) then
161         result := 1;
162       end if;
163     end if;
164   end loop;
165   end;
166   set_result(result);
167 end main;
```

Figure 5.3: The Copy Tool

5.5 An Example of a Distributed Program

In this section we present an example distributed program, by this we mean a program which explicitly communicates with a remote partner.

The file server provides a service whereby a named file may be executed. Programs on different machines may communicate by using the IPC but no direct, low-level mechanism is provided for remote program execution. The example illustrates how remote execution may be implemented at a higher level.

Any machine prepared to run programs on behalf of others executes a program which creates a Medium and associates it with a pathname in the file system. In the simplest case, this program will service requests which contain the pathname of the program to be executed. The following Ada program fragment, Figure 5.4, illustrates the principles involved.

```
procedure server is

  task type supervisor is
    ..
  end supervisor;

  tp : access_supervisor;

  task body supervisor is
  begin
    accept give_work(program_name_parameter) do
      program_name := program_name_parameter;
    end give_work;
    execute(program_name);  -- execute program by sending
                            -- request to local file server
  end supervisor;

begin
  channel_id := med_alloc;    -- create an IPC channel
  assert("/servers/remote_loader", channel_id);
  loop
    channel_id.receive_message(remote_request);
                            -- make a call on the buffer
                            -- task's receive entry

    tp := new supervisor;
    tp.give_work(remote_request.program_name);
  end loop;
end server;
```

Figure 5.4: Implementing Remote Execution - The Server

A more useful program might pass program parameters, input and output channels, and a current directory. Further enhancements might require a "logging in" procedure, might allow only a certain number of concurrent executions, or might accept a pathname relative to a default search path.

A user who wishes to use this service must himself use a tool to perform the necessary communication. The tool's parameters at least define the name of the program to be executed, and which particular server is expected to honour the request. Figure 5.5 gives a skeleton of a possible implementation.

```
procedure client is
begin
  channel_id := locate("/servers/remote_loader");
  read_my_arguments;
  channel_id.send_message(remote_request);
     -- make a call on the buffer task's send entry
end client;
```

Figure 5.5: Implementing Remote Execution - The Client

Alternatively the tool might itself be aware of a range of possible remote sites and may look for the first available.

Note that there is no explicit "machine" naming, rather the file pathname "/servers/remote_loader" is used to name the service provided by the server. The directory "/server" would typically be located on a third "central" (and presumably normally available) machine. A client may then discover which services are currently available by referencing a single remote machine.

5.6 Summary

PULSE offers users the basic facilities expected of any operating system: it also has primitives specific to its major design goals of supporting Ada, and distributed programming. Packages are provided to enable the user programmer to either avoid the distributed aspects of the system completely, or take explicit advantage of its message passing facilities. Unlike many systems, support is provided for parallel programming whereby individually scheduled tasks shared the same address space. This can aid the development of programs which contain inherent parallelism, but the programmer must be aware of its consequences.

6 THE PULSE KERNEL IMPLEMENTATION

6.1 Introduction

This chapter examines the actual implementation of the prototype PULSE kernel.

All but a small part of the kernel has been written in C[59]: LSI-11 assembly language has only been used when absolutely necessary. Ada was not chosen as the implementation language because its machine dependent features were not available in the York Compiler.

Figure 6.1 represents the implementation structure of the PULSE kernel. The remainder of this chapter will consider the individual layers.

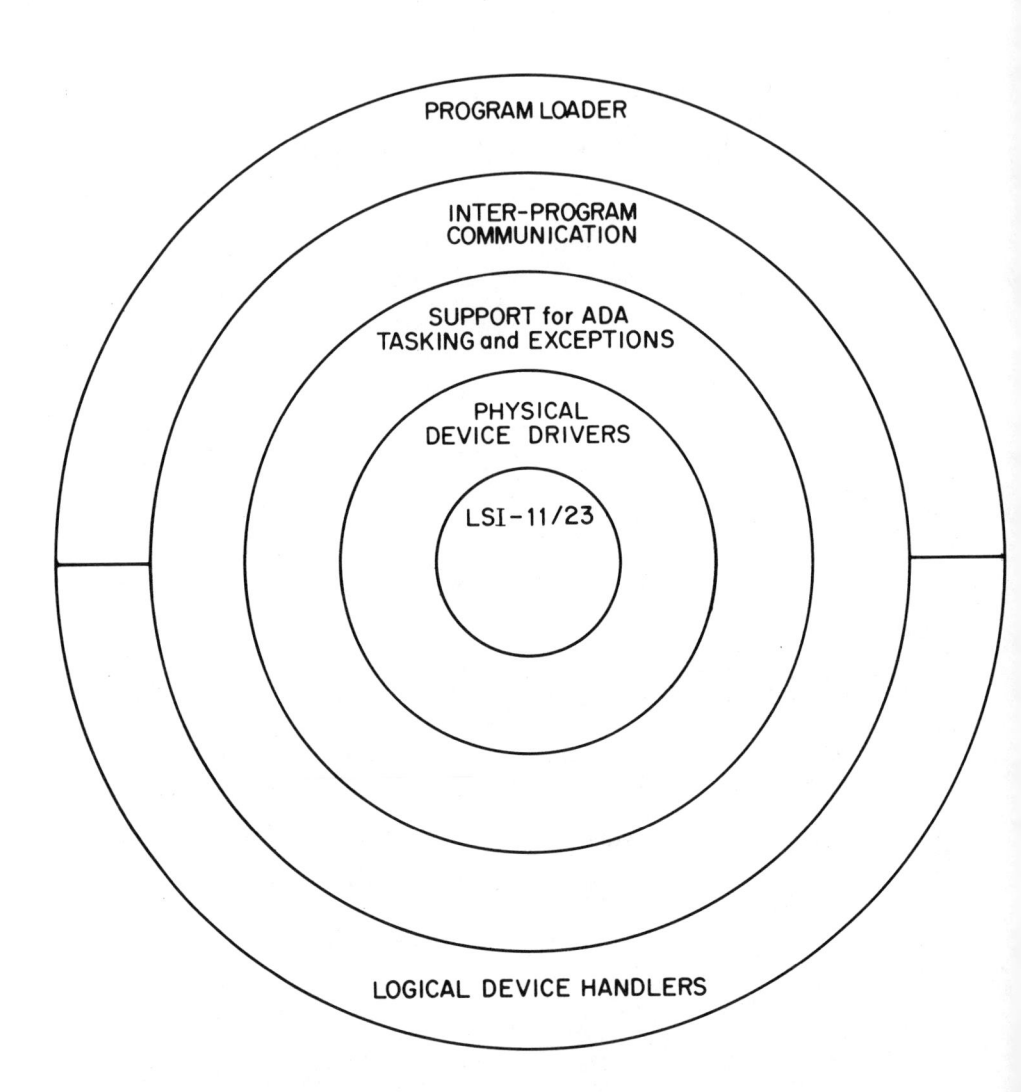

Figure 6.1: PULSE Kernel Implementation Layers

6.2 LSI-11/23

The LSI-11/23 has a 64k virtual address space and a 256k physical address space. This is not ideal for a PULSE machine, since any non-trivial use of Ada is likely to require a virtual address space larger than 64k. However, this machine was chosen as the hardware for the experiment because of its ready availability and the amount of accessible software*.

Both machines in the network have a terminal and an interrupt-driven Cambridge Ring interface. One of the machines has two DEC RP02 compatible 15 Mbyte disks and the other has a DEC RL02 compatible 8 Mbyte Winchester disk and a 1 Mbyte floppy disk.

6.3 Physical Device Drivers

Interrupts in PULSE are handled as procedural entries into the kernel. These procedures contain the basic device drivers. Programs outside the kernel may communicate with these drivers using the IPC. The Cambridge Ring Driver and its interface is described here as an example of this level of facility.

6.3.1 The Cambridge Ring Interface

The local area network which provides the communication subsystem is the Cambridge Data Ring[109]. Both the driver and basic block protocol[54] are built into the kernel.

The basic block protocol is a means of packaging useful blocks of data and providing a method of multiplexing their transmission and reception. Blocks are routed to logical 'ports' found at each station on the ring. Since a minipacket carries 16 bits of data, the term 'word' is applied here to mean 'minipacket'.

---

*The Department of Computer Science was already committed to producing a LSI/11-23 code generator for Ada.

A basic block commences with a header word of the form:

```
(bits)   4   2   10
       [ A | B |  C  ]
```

Where:

Field A is the binary pattern 1001.

Field B is the type of block:
 00 is a long block with end-around carry checksum;
 01 is a long block with checksum zero;
 10 is a single packet carrying data C;
 11 is an octet block with checksum.

If the block is a long block of type 00 or 01, it consists of:

a header word,
a route word,
C+1 data words and
a checksum word.

Type 11 blocks consist of:

a header packet, with C value 099 (hex);
a size word S;
a route word;
S+1 data octets;
checksum word.

The port identifier is contained in the route packets.

The basic block protocol is used with the added limitation that port identifiers are no more than 8 bits long. In the current implementation only type 0 blocks are used.

6.4 Support for Ada Tasking and Exception Handling

Because PULSE supports Ada programs in which tasks are scheduled individually the kernel needs to maintain status information on those tasks as well as the state of the program as a whole. Associated with each task is a task control block (TCB) which contains all the information required when the program in which it is active is swapped out. This includes the status of the task and its entries. There is also a "per task user area" which contains information about the state of the task when it is executing in kernel mode; this includes the kernel stack.

Associated with each program is a table containing information such as the value of the LSI-11/23 segmentation registers and a pointer to the first TCB. The relationship between these tables is shown in Figure 6.2 below.

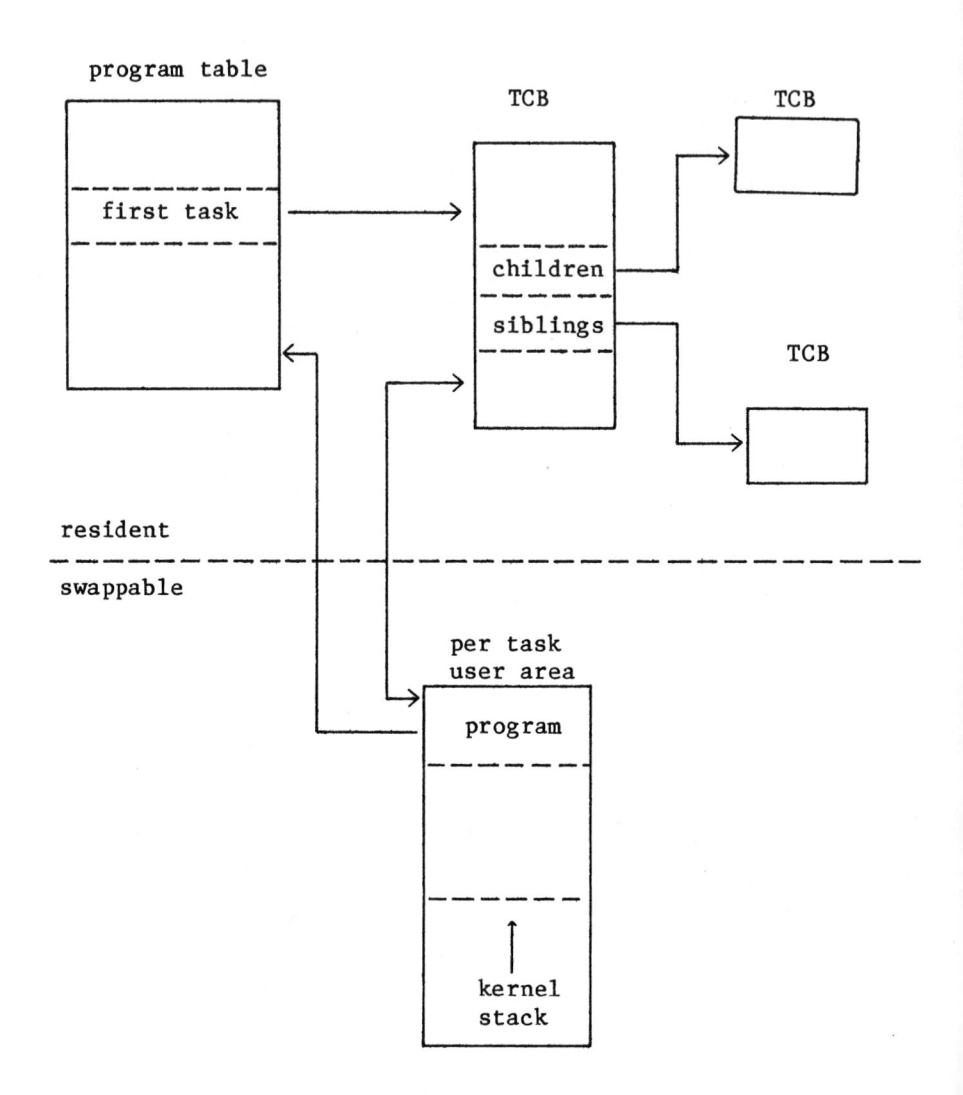

Figure 6.2: PULSE Kernel Tables

The storage layout of a program in core is given in Figure 6.3.

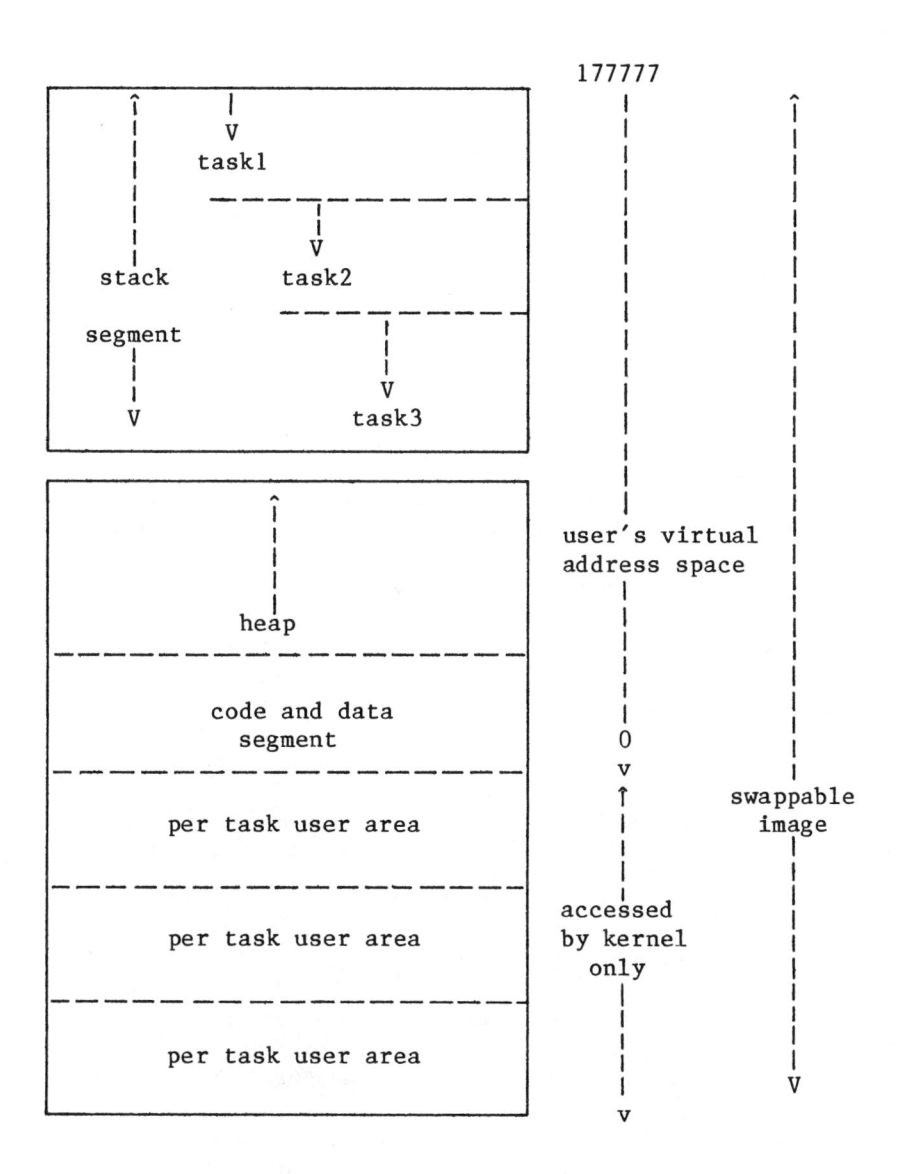

```
┌─────────────────────────────────┐                    177777
│    ↑     |                      │                      |              ↑
│    |     V                      │                      |              |
│    |   task1                    │                      |              |
│    |   — — — — — — — —          │                      |              |
│    |         |                  │                      |              |
│    |         V                  │                      |              |
│  stack     task2                │                      |              |
│ segment   — — — — — — —         │                      |              |
│    |             |              │                      |              |
│    |             |              │                      |              |
│    |             V              │                      |              |
│    V           task3            │                      |              |
└─────────────────────────────────┘                      |              |
┌─────────────────────────────────┐                      |              |
│         ↑                       │                  user's virtual     |
│         |                       │                  address space      |
│         |                       │                      |              |
│        heap                     │                      |              |
│  — — — — — — — — — — — —        │                      |              |
│                                 │                      |              |
│       code and data             │                      |              |
│         segment                 │                      0              |
│  — — — — — — — — — — — —        │                      v              |
│                                 │                      ↑       swappable
│     per task user area          │                      |         image
│                                 │                      |              |
│  — — — — — — — — — — — —        │                   accessed          |
│                                 │                  by kernel          |
│     per task user area          │                    only             |
│                                 │                      |              |
│  — — — — — — — — — — — —        │                      |              |
│                                 │                      |              |
│     per task user area          │                      |              V
│                                 │                      |
└─────────────────────────────────┘                      v
```

Figure 6.3: Core Layout of a PULSE Program

Each task requires two stacks, one in user and one in kernel space. The requirement for a user stack limits the number of tasks active at any moment, given the small virtual address space of an individual LSI-11/23 program. The size of each user stack may, however, be specified explicitly by the user program. However, neither the hardware nor the Ada compiler provides support for stack limit checking. Although the space for kernel stacks does not reside in a user program's address space, each requires a not inconsiderable amount of physical memory (1k from a total 248k).

When a task is executing in kernel mode, one of the kernel segmentation registers is set to point at the relevant per task user area.

6.4.1 Program Expansion

When a program needs to expand either because it must create a new task or because it needs more heap space, the kernel allocates space in memory for the new program image. The old image is then copied into the new space. For task creation space is required both for the new task's stack and the new task's per task user area.

If insufficient space is available then the program will be swapped out and only swapped in when a larger amount is available: this can cause considerable delay when a task is created.

6.4.2 Overlays

Due to the limited address space an overlaying facility is provided. This allows up to 8 segments of code to share the same virtual 8k page.

6.4.3 Rendezvous Support

The PULSE kernel incorporates a version of the suite of routines which provides support for the York Ada implementation[31]. The compiler assumes a number of routines to handle a standard entry call, a timed entry call, a conditional entry call, an accept, a select and task creation. These have been amended to allow more than one Ada program to be supported. No special facilities in the Ada compiler's code generator are required. Each routine is now split between the user's program and the kernel, and therefore results in a context switch. The code generator is not aware of this overhead and so there is no optimisation to keep the call of routines which require a trap into the kernel to a minimum. For example the current code generator generates a call to a control routine (postaccept) to indicate that an entry in a select statement is open and the calls a routine (select) to choose an entry to accept. A statement such as:

```
select
    accept A do
        S1;
    end accept;
    SA;
or
    accept B do
        S2;
    end accept;
        SB;
or
    accept do
        S3;
    end accept;
        SC;
end select;
```

will generate the following sequence of calls:

```
postaccept(A);
postaccept(B);
postaccept(C);
r = select;
case(r) of
1:
    S1;
    endaccept;
    SA;
2:
    S2;
    endaccept;
    SB;
3:
    S3;
    endaccept;
    SC;
end case;
```

Each of these calls will trap into the kernel. An improved use of control routines might simply generate a single routine call such as:

```
r = select(3,openarray);
case(r) of
1:
    S1;
    endaccept;
    SA;
2:
    S2;
    endaccept;
    SB;
3:
    S3;
    endaccept;
    SC;
end case;
```

where 3 is the number of branches in the select and the openarray is an array of bits which indicate which branches are open.

6.4.4 Task Scheduling

At present a simple three-level priority scheme is implemented. All tasks in the first executed program (the file system) have the highest (level 1) priority; all other tasks either have a foreground (level 2) or a background (level 3) priority. In the experimental implementation there is only crude time slicing: in general a task will run until it is blocked or until a higher priority task is runnable. A task may be blocked when it attempts to create a new task, requests a rendezvous with another task or a Medium task, or when it issues a "delay" request.

6.4.5 Exception Handling

The code for handling exceptions is split between the kernel and the user program. The kernel provides the routines for raising an exception and mapping hardware reported errors to standard exceptions. The code in the user program looks for and executes the handler and where necessary propagates the exception.

6.4.6 Limitations

In the prototype kernel implementation no attempt is made to reuse the per task user area or the stack of a task which has terminated. This results in programs which dynamically create and destroy tasks continually growing and quickly running out of address space. Even if the kernel did reuse this space the scope rules of Ada are such that tasks might not completely disappear when they terminate (see appendix C).

6.5 Inter-Program Communication(IPC)

6.5.1 Mediums

In chapter 2 the principles and high-level operation of the PULSE IPC were described. Here the concern is for the problems of its implementation. Programs are granted (and subsequently relinquish) Medium capabilities by issuing explicit requests: the relevant routines, "medalloc" and "meddealloc", are defined in the IPC package. A program which allocates a Medium has assigned to it read and write capabilities. It may at any time deallocate either or both capabilities. If the reader deallocates a Medium, that Medium is removed. An exception is raised in any writer which subsequently attempts to send a message to that Medium. If the reader dies after the writer has sent a message but before it has been read, no action is taken. If all writers to a Medium have deallocated that Medium, an exception will be raised in the reader task when it attempts to read any message from that Medium.

A task in one Ada program can pass on a write capability for a Medium to another Ada program by filling in the "reply" or "transfer" field in the message header. The system protects these capabilities so that only a writer can pass write capabilities, and so that a task which has no capability for a Medium cannot accidently pass one on. In the current implementation only the file system can pass a read capability to a program; this is further restricted by only allowing it to be done at program creation time. The problems of passing read capabilities across the network have yet to be investigated.

Although Mediums are conceptually buffer tasks, inside the kernel they are implemented as queues of messages.

Requests to a Medium are trapped by the kernel and the appropriate queue is accessed. If the number of messages in a queue reaches a defined maximum (one, in the current implementation) then any further request to send a message will be blocked until at least one message has been removed from the queue. If the total number of unread messages requires more than the space available in the kernel's buffers, then the messages may migrate to the swap area of the disk.

A Medium access variable is implemented differently from any normal task access variable. It is an index into an array of task access variables held by the system for that program. User programs are unaware of any difference.

6.5.2 Messages and their Structure

All messages have a header portion which contains a reply Medium descriptor, a transfer Medium descriptor and a user-supplied integer for reference. As Ada is a strongly typed language, data messages between programs are also typed. A message may be expressed in Ada as a variant record.

The data to be sent with a message are grouped together in units called data descriptors which are variant records whose discriminant defines the type of the data held by that unit. The kernel recognises a number of predefined data types which can be sent as valid data. They include variable length arrays of bytes, integers, characters, floats, Booleans and the capability to send and/or receive communication. In practice these facilities are not sufficient; a number of record structures have also been included to allow an efficient implementation of the file system. Also the concept of "unsafe data" transfer has been introduced to allow variable length and variable typed data to be received. Unsafe data is represented by a two field record structure. The first is the address of where the data is to be sent from or received into. The second field is the number of bytes to be sent or received. In the latter case it represents the maximum number of bytes the reader is prepared to receive. If the actual number is more, then only this number is received. If the actual number is less then the size field in the unsafe data is changed to reflect the actual number of bytes received.

Inter-Program Communication   95

If the reader sets the count in the unsafe data to 0, then the kernel simply fills in the number of bytes in the size field. The message once read, however, is left on the queue. This enables the reader to find out how much space is required, allocate the space and then reread the message.

A structured message consisting of more than one type can be sent by constructing a data descriptor which itself describes a variable length array of data descriptors.

Before a reader of a Medium can request data from that Medium, it must construct a message frame describing where the data must be stored. The system will then attempt to place the data in the area supplied by the reader.

6.5.3 Reply and Transfer Medium

Each message has two fields which can be used to transfer Medium capabilities. The act of sending the message grants write permission for the Mediums to the reader task.

6.5.4 Error Handling

There are three error conditions which can arise during the process of sending and receiving a message.

The first occurs when the program tries to access a Medium for which it does not have the correct capability. In this case an exception is raised from within the rendezvous and is propagated to the calling task.

The second error condition occurs when the reader of the Medium attempts to receive a message of a different type or subtype from the one that has been sent. Again, an exception is raised; however, the reader task may handle it and either send an error reply or simply deallocate any capabilities which may have been passed from the client program.

The third error condition is when a reader attempts to read from a Medium and there are no outstanding messages and no possible writer. The exception "no_writer" is raised. Similarly if a writer attempts to write to a Medium when there is no reader the exception "no_reader" is raised.

6.5.5 The Network Server

The network server provides a transparent extension to the IPC, permitting communication between PULSE machines. Messages are sent around the ring as basic blocks, without the imposition of any further message or protocol structure, apart from address translation, which is described later. In order to be able to forward a message to its proper destination, the driver keeps two tables. One, used when transmitting, is for mapping Medium identifiers to port numbers, and the other, used when receiving, is for mapping port numbers to Medium identifiers.* In either case the procedure is the same: the driver locates the 'source' value in the appropriate table and forwards the message to the corresponding 'destination'.

Start-up

Each machine has one port, the 'global' port, to which all other machines can send messages. It is used when each machine starts up, in the following way.

Initially each PULSE machine is not logically connected to the ring. When connection is desired, the relevant program (usually the file server) has to be granted a capability to write to the network server's external request Medium. This done, it will cause a Medium to be associated with the global port. The network server does this by entering the given Medium identifier and the global port number into the reception table. The program passes a local Medium identifier to the kernel which maps it to the relevant global identifier before passing it to the network server. The process of associating a Medium with a port has the effect of initialising the ring driver, thereby connecting the machine to the network.

---

*These tables are needed for proper recovery from crashes and should be kept in stable storage[64].

Address Translation

Once a machine is set up in this way, new table entries may be made when needed. To do this, the network server must examine the 'reply' field of any message passing through it. Outgoing messages must have their reply field changed from a Medium identifier to a port number, which must be allocated if necessary, and an entry for the Medium/port pair made in the reception table. Conversely, incoming messages must have their reply field changed from a port number to a Medium identifier, possibly with the allocation of a Medium, and again a table entry is made, this time in the transmission table.

Communication Failure

The network server makes no attempt at error correction, even though the basic block protocol has some error detection. If a corrupt message is received it is thrown away. Higher level software must timeout and retransmit the message.

In the current implementation no attempt is made to detect or recover from network or processor failure. Clearly detection is required in order to maintain the virtual circuit across machine boundaries. This is an area for future work.

6.6 Program Loading

On the LSI-11/23 a loaded program consists of two segments, code and data. To load a program the parent sends a "new program request" message to the kernel giving the sizes of the two segments. A zero code size indicates that the program is not sharable. The kernel creates space on the swap area, with a cleared data area, and returns a write capability for a Medium. This Medium is used by the parent to send to the kernel further messages concerning the child program. These messages contain requests for certain actions to be carried out on the loaded program. They are:

1) Load the following block of data at the specified virtual address in the program's virtual address space.

The kernel keeps no track of the quantity or location of the data it has loaded. It is also unaware of the file system commands which might be necessary to read the image from the local disk or across the network.

2) Start the program at the specified address with the given file system server and lifeline Mediums.

Each loaded program has four Mediums allocated to it at startup time. Two are used by the program for communication with the kernel, although for speed this communication is implemented as procedural entries into the kernel. The other two Mediums are used for communication with the file system and the real parent* of the new program, although their function is unknown to the kernel.

The 'start' message results in the user program being put on the run queue and being swapped in.

3) Raise the ABORT or BREAK exception in all tasks in the loaded program.

Neither of these exceptions can be trapped; however, the BREAK exception may be disabled.

4) Create another image of this program sharing its code.

The kernel will return write capabilities for a Medium which defines the new program. The parent program can then start to the new program and if necessary raise the ABORT or BREAK exception in it.

5) Read a block of data from the program's specified virtual address space.

The kernel reads the specified data and returns the data on the kernel reply Medium to that task.

---

*In PULSE all programs are executed by the File System in response to a user's program request. The lifeline is a link to the user's program which is termed the 'real parent'.

When the program terminates, it has the option of sending an exit status to the kernel. The kernel combines this status with its own status of the program when it terminates and sends it in a message to the parent program. The child program image remains until the parent deallocates its controlling Medium or until the parent also dies.

6.7 Logical Device Interface

The kernel manages physical devices such as the disk and the console. Any program which wishes to communicate with a kernel device must first request an appropriate Medium capability. It can then communicate with the kernel drivers to provide a logical interfaces for other programs.

6.8 Current Status

The current implementation of the PULSE kernel supports the following:

1) the running of multi-task Ada programs in separate address spaces and the handling of local exceptions;

2) the basic IPC which allows programs: to send and receive data messages (currently only a message queue of size 1 is implemented) with the passing on of reply and transfer capabilities, the sending of messages transparently across the network, and the raising of "no_reader" and "no_writer" exceptions except in the face of network partition and node failure;

3) the loading of non-sharable programs and

4) the accessing of the local disk and console devices.

The kernel consists of three segments: code (32k bytes, of which about 2k are generated from the assembly code), initialised data (4k) and uninitialised data (8k, mainly tables, including 2k general-purpose buffer space).

7 THE PULSE DISTRIBUTED FILE SYSTEM IMPLEMENTATION

7.1 Introduction

The file system is implemented by a single multi-task Ada program, termed the "file server", an instance of which runs on each PULSE machine. It is the first program executed by the PULSE kernel during the bootstrapping of the PULSE system. It runs in LSI-11/23 user mode and makes extensive use of the PULSE kernel's IPC mechanisms.

The file server provides two external interfaces, one to user programs termed the "public interface", and one to other (remote) instances of the file server termed the "private interface". The former provides a full UNIX-like file service including a hierarchical file store, access control, and the ability to load and execute a file. It allows users to request file operations in terms of both file pathnames and open files. Any such file operation may involve remote file access which is performed by the local file server via the private interface to other file servers. Pathnames are internally converted to lower-level unambiguous file identifiers termed "global i-numbers", and it is with these that the private interface is concerned.

Before embarking upon a description of the internal workings of the file server, it is instructive to describe, in some detail, the public interface and the constraints imposed on the implementation.

7.2 The Public Interface

User programs gain file system services solely via messages to their local file server, using its public interface. A fundamental assumption in the design of this interface is that Medium communication is reliable. Since the kernel, at present, only provides reliable message transmission between programs running on the same machine, user programs should not communicate with remote instances of the file server directly.

7.2.1 File Server Request Mediums

Each user program starts execution with a Medium write capability to what is termed its "file server request" Medium. This is a Medium owned by the file server, through which may be sent file system requests such as "open file", "change working directory" etc. Such a user program is termed a client of the file server's public interface. For each such current client the file server maintains a "client table entry" which is a record containing the corresponding file server request Medium and other information such as user identifier, working directory etc.

7.2.2 Open File Mediums

In response to a successful open file request the file system returns a write capability to a further "open file" Medium. The client sends further requests such as "read" and "write" through this Medium rather than the file server request Medium. This open file Medium identifies the particular open file to the file server, rather than a file descriptor as in UNIX. It is just like any other Medium and hence a client is free to pass on such a capability to another program.

7.2.3 Reply Mediums

Every client request includes a Medium capability through which the file server will send its reply. The file server cannot tell, and does not care, whether successive requests through a particular Medium are from the same client program. The file access protection provided by the file server thus relies on the kernel's guarantee that messages may not be sent to a Medium by an arbitrary unauthorised program.

7.2.4 Resource Deallocation

The file server is notified whenever a file server request or open file Medium is no longer in use since the kernel raises an exception in a task reading from a Medium which has no writers. On terminating, a program's Medium capabilities are automatically revoked and hence its open files (assuming it has not passed on any capabilities to them), are closed, and resources associated with its file server request Medium released. Alternatively a file may be closed at any time simply by explicitly deallocating its Medium capability.

7.2.5 Program Execution

The most complex part of the public interface is that concerned with program execution. The file server provides a service whereby a named file may be executed, subject to access control permission as in UNIX. One client, the "parent", may invoke a further program, its "child". The parent may wait, unlike UNIX, only for a named child to terminate, when it will receive an exit status. Furthermore a parent may modify the environment of the child, prior to its execution. This is achieved by manipulating file server request Mediums as follows. A "clone" request may be sent through a file server request Medium. On receipt of this the file server allocates a new file server request Medium and associated client table entry, copying details such as user identifier and working directory from the original entry. The client program now has two "identical" file server request Mediums, to which he may direct similar kinds of requests. The only difference is that the new "cloned" Medium may also be sent an "execute program" request. This causes a named file to be executed with a fresh file server request Medium whose client table entry has attributes copied from that associated with the "cloned" Medium, which itself is deallocated. These attributes, such as working directory, may differ from the original as they may have been altered since the "clone" operation. Moreover the effective user id may be inherited, not from the "cloned" Medium, but from the executable program file. This implements the UNIX setuid facility since the parent has no access to its child's file server request Medium.

The parent program may wait for the child by issuing a "wait" request to its original file server request Medium.

Since it is the file server that actually requests the kernel to execute a new program, explicitly loading the code having first read it from disk or across the network from another file server, the file server is notified by the kernel when the program terminates with an indication of any abnormal termination. The file server combines this exit status with an explicit return status which may be sent by the child through its file server request Medium, and includes it in a reply to the parent's outstanding wait request.

As well as a write capability to the file server a new program also commences with a read capability for his so-called "lifeline" Medium. The file server arranges that the parent is given a write capability to this Medium, parent and child can thus communicate independently of the file server. Conventionally the parent sends the child its parameters through the lifeline, these consist of an arbitrary number of strings and the standard I/O open file Medium capabilities. An open file passed on in this way is equivalent to a UNIX file inherited at process creation, i.e. fork time. Two programs may hence share the read/write pointer to a single file, and the file server does not close the file until each program has finished using it.

These mechanisms allow the PULSE shell to execute programs in a similar way to the UNIX shell, even though PULSE provides a completely different tasking model from that of UNIX. Furthermore the file server itself executes in LSI-11 user mode using the same kernel IPC mechanisms as other programs, yet provides a UNIX-like service to those programs.

7.2.6 Distribution and Replication

Apart from a few specific operations, the facilities provided by the file server's public interface involve no notion of file distribution or replication. All programs, except those utilities that manipulate duplicate files, may ignore these matters. A minor exception is the PULSE shell, which uses the "set_map" request to influence the file server's file selection mechanism.

7.3 Implementation Constraints

The file server is written almost completely in Ada. To enable portions of the file server to be tested under UNIX, a few packages have alternative bodies, written in C, to interface to underlying UNIX facilities.

7.3.1 Ada Language Constraints

Major Ada features not used due to lack of (timely) compiler implementation include generics, private types and derived types. The generic procedures unchecked_deallocation and unchecked_conversion were required and therefore simulated using overloaded references to two C functions. Less important unimplemented features which would have proved useful include indexed components of function call results, long integers and subunits.

In the absence of long integers, a few trivial C functions were written to allow an integer to be manipulated as an unsigned value. These functions, along with the functions to implement unchecked deallocation and conversion, are the only non-Ada code in the file server when it is supported by the PULSE kernel.

7.3.2 Restrictions on Use of Tasking

The most important features of Ada used by the file server are those related to tasking. Tasking is used extensively to enable each active file server to service several requests (from both public and private interfaces), concurrently. No assumptions are made concerning the underlying implementation of tasking, except that continuous dynamic creation and termination of tasks is impractical, and that tasks are "expensive". The former constraint arises because stack space for terminated tasks is not re-used. The reasons for tasks being "expensive" in their memory requirements are now outlined.

7.3.2.1 Task Storage Overhead

Each task requires two stacks, one in user and one in kernel space. The requirement of a user stack limits the total number of tasks active at any moment, given the small virtual address space of an individual LSI-11/23 program. The size of each user stack may, however, be specified explicitly by the user program. The file server makes use of the facility to minimise the size of user stacks. However, since neither the hardware nor the Ada compiler provides support for stack limit checking, this facility is a mixed blessing. Although the space for kernel stacks does not reside in a user program's address space, each requires a not inconsiderable amount of physical memory (1k from a total 248k). Moreover, the kernel's representation of an executing program demands that all kernel stacks be contiguously present in core whenever an individual task is executing. This can cause considerable delay when a task is created whilst the kernel finds space for the new, larger, program image (see section 6.4 Support for Ada Tasking and Exception Handling).

7.3.3 Dynamic Storage Allocation

As well as being careful about storage allocated statically to tasks, the file server must be careful about other storage requirements, since it runs "for ever". Ada enforces the use of a heap for dynamic storage allocation and the file server takes the responsibility of explicitly returning storage when necessary. Space for tables and messages is allocated from the heap during package and task elaborations, and never returned. No attempt is made to recover from a possible "storage_error" exception during initialisation, the assumption being that the table sizes must be too large or too many tasks have been initiated. In certain cases, during remote file access, space for messages is allocated from the heap on demand, and must therefore be explicitly deallocated using unchecked_deallocation subprograms. Lack of space in this situation is treated as a transient error. For situations where a task requires space dynamically but is prepared to wait for another task to free space, the disk buffer management package provides the ability to allocate and free anonymous disk block size chunks of store.

7.3.4 Overlays

Despite the measures taken to minimise space requirements, the file server soon ran out of address space as new facilities were added. To allow further development, an overlaying facility was incorporated into the kernel. This allows up to 8 segments of code to share the same virtual 8k page. Extra code could then be added to the file server, at the run-time cost of a trap into the kernel whenever control passes between overlay segments, and a further reduction in physical memory available to other programs.

7.3.5 Task Synchronisation Overhead

Finally the run-time cost of communication between tasks must be considered. The time taken to perform a rendezvous is at best 5 milliseconds (see section 8.1). Task communication is hence very costly compared, say, with subprogram calls. Any comparison with the implementation of similar features in the UNIX kernel must take into account the radically different synchronisation mechanisms employed.

7.4 File Server Structure

The file server is organised as two Ada libraries, mainly to ease concurrent development by two programmers. One library, termed "high", concerns itself with the public interface calling upon the services of the other library when necessary. That library, termed "low", concerns itself with implementing file operations. It does this, on behalf of tasks in the "high" library, by utilising local disks and by communicating with remote servers when necessary. It also performs file operations utilising local disks on behalf of remote file servers. The "low" library thus provides the "private" interface to its local resources, and uses the "private" interface to access remote resources. It provides a subprogram interface to the "high" library, and provides and uses a message interface for communication with remote instances of itself.

Each library contains several packages; the division into library packages is partly for logical structuring, and partly for pragmatic reasons of separate compilation. The use of subunits for separate compilation was not considered as they were not implemented in the compiler when the file server was written.

7.4.1 Use of Tasking

When an Ada task is waiting for an IPC message, the PULSE kernel is able to schedule another task in the same program. This means that the file server may make extensive use of Ada tasks in order to service several client requests in parallel. Incoming requests are serviced by individual tasks, one for each outstanding Medium. These tasks exist for the life of the file server, their number being determined at compile time. Other tasks are used to synchronise access to shared data, for instance each on-line disk volume is controlled by its own task. Physical I/O is performed by directing requests through a Medium owned by the kernel; a special optimisation allows DMA disk transfers to be performed.

It is useful to classify file server tasks into three kinds, "worker", "controller", and "manager".

A worker task performs work in response to messages sent through a Medium owned by the file server. Such messages are termed "requests" and such Mediums "request Mediums". A program which sends such a request is termed a client of the file server, it may be a user program or another instance of the file server. Having processed a request a worker task sends a single "reply" message through a "reply Medium" owned by the client. The types of messages which the file server handles are defined in the **pulse_ipc** package. The file server declares a "worker" task type for each such type of message. A fixed number of worker tasks of each type is created when the file server starts up, and each such task is limited to handling requests of a single message type. Should a client send a request message of the wrong type, an exception is raised within the worker task when it attempts to receive the message. Likewise an exception is raised in the client if it attempts to receive its reply into a message structure of the wrong type. This gives a limited a form of run-time type checking.

Each worker task type has an associated "controller" task. The controller's function is to allocate work to individual worker tasks. The "work" to be done by a worker task is effectively defined by the "request Medium" through which it receives client requests. A worker may receive this Medium from its controller, or allocate it itself. In either case it repeatedly receives and services requests from that Medium until there are no writers to the Medium, or an explicit termination request is received. The worker then makes an entry on its controller to request further work.

To service an individual request, a worker task calls on subprograms within various packages. Some packages contain data which must not be accessed concurrently by two or more worker tasks. A "manager" task, sometimes hidden within the package body, controls access to such shared data.

7.5 The Library High

The library "high" consists of packages which implement the public interface, by calling on "low" library packages where necessary.

The file server request manager, is the major package within the "high" library. It is concerned with the file server request Mediums, described in section 7.2, and contains the worker tasks which receive requests and an associated controller task. The controller task has two entries, **give_work** and **new_client**. A worker task is assigned work by calling the entry **give_work**, which returns a client table entry, containing a file server request Medium. The client table is a data structure defined elsewhere. The basic structure of a file server request worker task is shown in Figure 7.1.

```
loop
    controller.give_work(client);
    begin
       loop
          client.fsr_medium.receive_message(request);
          case request.request_code is
             when  OPEN  => do_open;
             when  CLONE => do_clone;
                    .
                    .
                    .
          end case;

          request.reply.send(reply);
          meddealloc(request.reply);
       end loop;
    exception
       when NO_WRITER => null;  --* client finished
    end;
end loop;
```

Figure 7.1: File Server Worker Task Structure

Having received a client table entry "client" from the controller, the worker then repeatedly receives messages on its file server request Medium and replies until there are no writers left, when it returns for more work. The body of the controller is shown in Figure 7.2

```
loop
   accept give_work(client : out p_client_t) do
      accept new_client(caller: p_client_t) do
         client := caller;
      end new_client;
   end give_work;
end loop;
```

Figure 7.2: Controller Task's Body

The controller just waits for a worker to indicate it is ready to be assigned a fresh client table entry, and gets that entry by performing a further, nested, accept.

As indicated in the worker task code fragment above, each file server request is handled by an individual subprogram. Some operations, such as "set_map", are trivial requiring simply the setting or retrieving of a value in the client table entry. Others, such as "link" and "unlink", are more complicated and call on file managing packages in the "low" library. These packages, however, provide similar functions to those in the UNIX kernel, and hence most of the subprograms are modelled on their UNIX equivalents. Issues of distribution and replication are, for the most part, invisible at this level.

7.5.1 Open Files

Each open file is handled by a worker task, dedicated to servicing requests to the open file Medium by which that open file is identified externally, as explained in section 7.2. These worker tasks, and their associated controller task, are contained within a package which has a subprogram interface.

The subprograms which open and create files first locate the named file by calling the function **namei** from the "low" library package **naming** (see section 7.6.4). This returns an "i-node pointer" which is a handle on the file and explained in detail later; suffice to say that further "low" functions are available to read, write etc. its associated file. The UNIX semantics of "create file" are preserved in that the named file is opened, having first been truncated if it already exists and created otherwise.

If the file is successfully located or created then a worker task is assigned and a freshly allocated Medium (the open file Medium), an "i-node pointer", and an indication of whether the file is opened for reading or writing (or both) are passed to it. Having been given some work the open file task repeatedly receives requests from its open file Medium. Requests to read and write from/to the file are carried out by way of calling appropriate "low" subprograms and packaging the results up in a reply message. Eventually the worker task discovers that the file is to be closed by the absence of writers to its Medium. It then calls an appropriate "low" subprogram to "deactivate" the i-node and returns to its controller to request more work.

Note that there is no global or per client "open file table" such as in the UNIX kernel[101]. The ability to pass on open file Mediums between programs obviates the need for the former, and the existence of a task for each open file the latter. The only limit on the number of files an individual client may have is determined by the general limit on his Medium capabilities, assuming of course that the file server has enough resources. No further restriction seems necessary in a personal computer environment.

7.6 The Library Low

The library "low" concerns itself solely with the internal implementation of "files". As in UNIX its activities centre around the concept of an i-node[101]. Several alternative methods of implementing the operations on i-nodes were considered. The solution chosen was to emulate the UNIX kernel for local access by representing each active i-node by an entry in a table, and provide a subprogram interface whereby the work is done by the calling task. Remote file access is achieved by allowing a table entry to represent a "remote" active i-node. Each subprogram which implements an i-node operation first checks whether the i-node is remote and if so calls a subprogram in a further package which implements a "remote procedure call" interface to remote file servers.

An alternative method would have been to communicate solely via a message interface. Each active i-node would have been represented by a Medium within a worker task, much as open files are implemented. Even for local file access it would be this worker task, rather than a task in the "high" library, which performed the work. These i-node worker tasks could be in a different program to the "high" library tasks, which would send messages regardless of whether files were remote or local.

The former approach was adopted, mainly because it allowed much testing of the file server to be done before Medium communication was implemented. It is also, however, less demanding in resources such as tasks and Medium capabilities, and allows local file access to be performed more efficiently due to less data copying, message passing and context switching. On the debit side, the adopted method requires the implementation of separate local and remote interfaces to the i-node operations, and forces the file server to be a single program with the attendant space problems.

We may consider four distinct levels of abstraction within the implementation of files.

1) At the bottom level the disk buffer cache provides operations on physical disk blocks, identified by local physical device plus disk block address.

2) The disk volume level provides globally identified structured disk volumes, with the facility to allocate and free disk blocks and local i-numbers.

3) The active i-node level utilises the buffer cache, the disk volume level and also remote instances of itself, to provide the notion of an active i-node to which may be directed requests such as "read/write n bytes at file offset x". This level incorporates a mapping from a "global i-number" to a physical i-number which defines the particular instance of the i-node selected. It thus implements both replication and distribution.

4) At the top-most level, the textual naming of files is provided. The concept of a directory is implemented utilising the active i-node level to read and write directory files. The global hierarchical file store is

implemented by providing a mapping from pathname to active i-node. At this level the existence of multiple copies of a file and its location are hidden, as are all details of its storage.

We now discuss these levels in detail.

7.6.1 The Disk Buffer Cache

The package **buff_io** provides a subprogram interface to the disk buffer cache. It maintains a set of disk block sized buffers, each of which may be temporarily associated with a physical disk block. A task gains exclusive access to a particular disk block, unconditionally waiting if it is already in use. Subprograms are available to read and write the data in the buffer to the corresponding disk block. **Buff_io** is essentially an Ada implementation of the UNIX block I/O system[101], the main difference being that the actual disk I/O is performed by sending messages to the kernel, rather than initiating interrupt driven subprograms as in the UNIX kernel. Callers of the package are assumed to be well behaved in that they return the correct buffer after a short time; no provision is built in to detect incorrect usage such as returning an old buffer not now allocated, or holding two buffers within a re-entrant subprogram, which may lead to deadlock.

7.6.1.1 Buffer Representation

Each buffer has a header and a body. A header is represented by a record which contains a pointer to a buffer body, represented by a disk block size array of bytes. Both buffer header and body space is allocated from the heap at package elaboration time. A manager task controls access to the buffers, searching the buffer queues and manipulating them under mutual exclusion. The caller is returned a pointer to a buffer header from which he may derive the pointer to the buffer body itself. No other access to the buffer header should be made by the caller. Clearly the buffer header could be implemented as a private type to enforce this rule, and a function be provided to return the buffer body associated with a given buffer header. This approach was rejected due to the compiler's inability to support indexed components of a function call result, and the overhead in time and space which would be incurred by the extra function call.

7.6.1.2 Buffer Allocation

A rendezvous with the buffer manager task is required to both get and free a buffer. The entry call **get**, which is made by the package's public subprogram **get_buff** to get a buffer on behalf of its caller, returns a buffer header and an indication of whether the buffer is busy. If so then a further entry call is made on the manager to one of the family of entries **wait**, the index of which indicates which buffer is being waited for. At least one rendezvous is therefore required to either get or free a buffer. This scenario ignores the more complicated case of a request for a disk block that is not in the cache when all buffers are busy.

7.6.1.3 Physical I/O

Any I/O required is performed by the public subprograms, to or from an allocated buffer body. Communication with a disk driver is synchronous, in that on returning from sending the message the kernel has already performed the I/O. The calling task is held whilst the kernel performs a DMA transfer from the file server's address space to the disk. This is a non-standard mechanism which simplifies access to devices but makes parallelism hard to achieve. Because of this, read ahead is not implemented and write behind is achieved by delaying writing a "dirty" buffer until it is needed to store a different disk block, at which point the requesting task is held for the duration of the disk write.

7.6.1.4 Limits to Parallelism

Parallelism close to that achieved by the UNIX kernel, which efficiently overlaps disk I/O time, cannot be achieved by introducing further tasks since a rendezvous time of at least 5 milliseconds would probably defeat any prospective gains. A more elegant implementation of the disk cache manager might associate a task with each buffer. In this solution the buffer task itself does the I/O and communicates the results to the calling task via a rendezvous. This solution was not adopted due to the prospective overhead both in time and space. An alternative solution might be for the kernel to support an interrupt entry mechanism to indicate message delivery, in this case the completion of an I/O request, but this is a non-trivial mechanism.

7.6.1.5 Rendezvous Optimisation

In the current implementation the manager task emulates a monitor, whereby the entries are called under mutual exclusion, and entry family indices serve as condition variables. In such a task it is theoretically possible to dispense with the context switch needed to perform a rendezvous[37]. In the absence of a compiler able to perform such an optimisation, a version of **buff_io** was constructed which does the optimisation by hand, as it were, relying on a non-preemptive scheduling strategy (the file server executes at the highest priority) to guarantee mutual exclusion when executing the manager's entry code in the caller's context. This reduces the cost of getting or freeing a block when no waiting is involved to be that of a single subprogram call. This was done after the file server was operational and resulted in a noticeable increase in performance, particularly program loading when many disk blocks are read in quick succession, two rendezvous being avoided for every block.

7.6.2 Disk Volumes

This level supports the notion of a structured disk volume.

7.6.2.1 Disk Volume Layout

The format of a PULSE disk volume is similar to that of a UNIX "file system"[101]. The first block (address 0) is reserved for a possible bootstrap. The next block (address 1) is the so-called "super block". This contains the same information as a UNIX "super block", for example the disk size and the size of sub-regions of the disk. It also contains the volume's identifier, which indicates whether the volume is a master or duplicate, and the range of global i-numbers assigned to this volume. Next comes the "i-list", a number of blocks containing the i-nodes i.e. file definitions. Following this region, for duplicate volumes only, comes the "i-map". This occupies several blocks, and may be viewed as a large array, each item of which corresponds to a global i-number. If the entry is zero then the file corresponding to that global i-number is not currently duplicated. If non-zero then it is the local i-number of the duplicate file's i-node. Between the end of the i-list (or i-map for duplicate volumes) and the end of the disk come free blocks which may be assigned to individual files.

Free space on a volume is maintained by a linked list of available disk blocks, just as in UNIX. Blocks are assigned to individual files by means of a list of disk addresses in the i-node, as in UNIX. The first few (7 at present, 10 in UNIX) of these point directly at the first few blocks of the file. There follows an array of three "indirect" blocks, which are used for single, double and triple "indirect" addresses. At present only single indirect addressing is implemented since the maximum file size is limited by the size of an integer to 32k.

7.6.2.2 Disk Volume Mounting

The package **disk_vol** provides routines to mount and dismount physical disk devices as disk volumes, and to search the table of local on-line volumes which it maintains. This table includes both the physical device and volume identifier of each volume currently on-line.

Each on-line volume has an associated manager task which maintains the in-core copy of the volume's "super block", writing it out periodically (every 30 seconds at present) and when the volume is dismounted. As in UNIX the "super block" contains the start of the free data block list and the complete free i-number list. The manager task provides mutually exclusive access to these lists by offering entries to allocate and free data blocks and i-numbers. As the free i-number and free block lists are independent each could have its own manager task to increase parallelism.

7.6.3 The Active I-node Level

The package **inode** contains the active i-node table itself and a task to synchronise access to the table, and provides as public subprograms the basic operations on active i-nodes.

7.6.3.1 Package Inode's User Interface

This is modelled on that used in the UNIX kernel, operations being available to get (or activate), lock, release, and put (or deactivate) i-nodes. An i-node is activated by calling **iget** with parameters of a global i-number, a boolean indicating whether access is for update, and a client table entry pointer. The latter two parameters influence which specific instance of the file is located. Only those cases set in the client table's "file_map" field are considered, and of those only the master file cases if access for update is specified. Local subprogram **specific_iget** is called to activate a particular instance of a file. In all cases **iget** returns a pointer, possibly null, to a locked i-node table entry. This i-node pointer can then be presented to further routines to perform other operations, more interesting ones such as read and write being defined within other packages. The caller may discover, by inspecting the i-node table entry, which particular instance of the file has been located. Any direct reference to the table entry's data i.e. the i-node itself, should be performed under mutual exclusion, for which purposes the ability to lock and release the entry are provided. The locking is at present, as in UNIX, conservative, guaranteeing exclusive use regardless of whether or not access is for update. The caller need not be concerned whether the located file is remote or local.

7.6.3.2 Duplicate File Synchronisation

If **iget** returns a duplicate i-node then synchronisation, if needed, has already been performed. **Iget** activates both master and duplicate copies of the file by calling local subprogram **specific_iget**, then calls a routine to update the duplicate version.

7.6.3.3 I-node Table Manager Task

The i-node table manager task, follows a similar model to the buffer manager task. An entry **igrab** is provided to look through the i-node table for a given file instance under mutual exclusion. If the entry is already locked then the calling (internal) routine must retry using the entry family **wait**, whose index identifies a particular table entry. If the search fails then a free slot is returned. If the table is full and the search fails then failure is reported. Note the difference to the buffer manager in which a caller may wait for a buffer to be freed. I-nodes are freed less frequently, moreover the calling task may wish to have several active i-nodes concurrently. Forcing the caller to get them all immediately, or give up, eliminates the possibility of deadlock due to mutual embraces.

As mentioned earlier, the locking strategy is conservative. In a distributed environment this means remote file access can cause local access to wait for a relatively long time. For instance, if a file server is loading a remote program, then that program file's i-node is locked whilst its data is transferred between machines; an attempt to concurrently execute the program on its own machine is held up until it has been loaded on the other machine. The problem may be alleviated somewhat by implementing a single writer, multiple readers locking strategy. Such a facility could be incorporated into the i-node table manager task straightforwardly without addition of extra task entry specifications. Note must be taken if an i-node is locked for reading or writing, and a release of a write lock must cause those waiting on the entry family index to retry, with the possibility of waiting writers having to try again if a reader gets the lock first.

As in the buffer manager package, a version of the **inode** package has been constructed which executes the manager task's accept code in the context of the calling task in certain (common) cases.

7.6.3.4 Remote Active I-nodes

Remote files are allocated i-node table entries in the same manner as local files. The only difference is that the i-node data is read from a remote file server whenever a lock operation is performed, and written back whenever a release is performed after such an i-node has been changed. A remote i-node is flagged as such in the i-node table, and contains a Medium capability through which to communicate with a remote file server's i-node worker task (termed a "remote i-node" Medium), a local Medium capability used to receive replies, and pointers to two appropriate message structures. These resources are allocated dynamically when an i-node table entry is assigned to a remote i-node, and released when the remote i-node has no more local users. Two or more tasks wishing to activate the same remote i-node, share the remote i-node table entry as if it were local. The remote i-node itself is only put (deactivated) when there are no more local users.

Every subprogram which operates on an active i-node first checks to see if it is remote, and if so calls a corresponding subprogram in the package **rino_cl**, i.e remote i-node client. This package uses the "private interface" to other instances of the file server, to implement the file operations that, for local files, are provided by accessing local disks.

7.6.3.5 Logical File I/O

The package **ilevel_io** provides subprograms to read and write to a given active i-node. For local file access this involves calling the function to convert a logical block address to a physical block number. **Buff_io** is then used to perform the disk transfers.

Readi and **writei** provide the ability to read and write an arbitrary amount of data from an arbitrary offset in the file. The caller specifies a core address to indicate where the data is to go/come to/from. These routines perform the "smoothing" of transfers across disk block boundaries. When used by the "high" library to implement the user "read" and "write" requests, this resulted in data being copied between the buffer cache and file worker task buffers, before being sent to the client as a message. The file workers could only afford a limited size buffer, originally 64 bytes. This resulted in 8 client requests being sent just to read a single block from a file.

To overcome this problem, further subprograms were introduced to deal in disk cache buffer pointers rather than core addresses. A corresponding facility for writing is also provided. The problem arises, however, that the file worker task does not know that he has to perform a write request until he has received the data to be written. He therefore must allocate local buffer space for the largest potential write. To overcome this problem a kernel facility was added to "unsafe data" type messages to allow a reader of a message to not accept the actual data in an unsafe message until he knows its size.

These rather messy changes increased the speed of file access greatly, and eliminated the need for the file worker tasks to have their own data buffers. Care is taken that the callers need not know whether the file they are reading/writing is local or remote.

7.6.3.6 The Private Interface

The private interface between file servers is provided by the package **rino_serv**, i.e. remote i-node server, and utilised by the package **rino_cl**, i.e. remote i-node client. Between them, they provide what is effectively a "remote procedure call" interface to the package **inode**. Thus when servicing a request from a client of its public interface, the file server may itself become a client of a remote file server's private interface. In this section "client" thus refers to a file server rather than a user program.

Rino_serv contains a number of worker tasks, each of which request work from a controller task. The controller task receives requests from its machine's "global Medium" (see section 4.3.1) of two kinds, either "locate volume" or "activate i-node". In both cases a global i-number "n" is included as a parameter to the request. The former request means "do you have on-line the volume which contains the i-node identified by n". If it is on-line the controller returns a further Medium capability to the global Medium in a reply message. The reply also contains the disk volume identifier (see section 7.6.2.1 above) of the located volume. If unsuccessful it sends no reply and simply returns to receive a further message from the "global Medium".

When it receives an "activate i-node" request the controller passes the message on as "work" to a worker task. The worker task activates the i-node, if possible, using the local **inode** package, and replies to the client with Medium capability to a new "remote i-node Medium". The worker task then repeatedly receives messages through this Medium and performs the appropriate request by utilising the local **inode** package subprograms.

Requests to "get" (activate) or "lock" the i-node are executed by performing the equivalent local operation, then returning the i-node data itself in the reply message. A request to "release" or "put" the i-node may contain i-node data which is copied into the local i-node table. Upon receipt of a "put" (deactivate) request, the worker calls the local **inode** package **iput** procedure, deallocates its Medium capabilities, then returns to the manager for more work.

If at any time a worker fails to communicate with its client, for example due to the client having explicitly or implicitly deallocated its "remote i-node" Medium capability, then the worker acts as if a "put" request with no i-node data had been received. Hence the "put" request is not strictly necessary since the client may achieve the same effect by an "irelease" followed by the deallocation of its capability to the "i-node" Medium. The "put" request, however, allows the worker to distinguish between intended and unintended termination of activity, the latter case being possible due to a crash of the client's machine or a bug in its software. Furthermore, it requires less inter-machine message traffic.

Rino_cl contains a subprogram for each active i-node operation. Most of these subprograms are straight forward; they simply use the data in an active i-node table entry for a remote i-node to perform the operations provided by the private interface. The initial activation of a remote active i-node is, however, more complex than subsequent actions. The subprogram **client_iget** accesses a remote machine by sending a "locate volume" message to its own machine's "broadcast Medium" (see section 4.3.1), including the global i-number "n" of the file of interest as a parameter. This message is delivered to the controller tasks of the **rino_server** package in other file servers, as described above. At most, one remote file server replies to indicate it has the volume on-line and provides a further Medium for future communication. A message is then sent to that Medium requesting the activation of the particular i-node (identified by global i-number). This results, if successful, in a further "remote i-node" Medium capability being returned which is stored in a local active i-node table entry.

Rino_cl maintains a "remote on-line volume table", containing disk volume identifiers and corresponding Medium capabilities, to enable the first stage of the above process to be avoided when a further i-node is to be activated on the same remote volume.

7.6.3.7 Communication Protocol

Unlike the public interface, the private interface assumes the use of "unreliable" Mediums. By this we mean that file servers communicate via Mediums through which messages are not guaranteed to be delivered, but those that are delivered are intact and in order. All requests between the file servers are carefully designed to be repeatable. This enables the client (i.e. the **rino_cl** package executing within a remote instance of the file server) to apply a simple protocol to take account of lost messages. Reading and writing data from a given offset in the file are simple examples of repeatable transactions. Any repeat of such an operation is invisible to the server which just performs the action as usual. Locking and releasing the i-node are slightly trickier, the server must, for instance, be aware that the i-node is locked and ignore a repeated request. The initial activation of the i-node is perhaps the most awkward case. No special arrangements are made, the argument to support the correctness of this approach is as follows.

First we present the normal protocol applied by the client to cope with lost messages.

1) The client assigns a "transaction number" and stores it in the request message's "my reference" header field.

2) The client sends the request.

3) The client waits for a reply, discarding messages whose "my reference" header field does not match the transaction number, and deallocating any Medium capabilities contained therein.

4) If the reply has not been received within a timeout period, then steps (ii) and (iii) are repeated, giving up after a certain number of retries.

The worker just receives requests and sends replies on a one to one basis, remembering to copy the transaction number from the incoming request message to the outgoing reply.

A further protocol is involved when activating an i-node. The client sends a "get" request and includes a "i-node reply" Medium capability. The server's worker task stores this Medium and uses it for all future replies, up to and including a reply to a "put" (deactivate) request. His reply to the "get" includes an "i-node request" Medium capability, through which further i-node requests are expected to be sent.

Now consider a request to activate an i-node. A worker task is allocated, the i-node is locally activated and locked, and a reply sent. The client however may timeout in waiting for the reply and repeat the request. A request for the very i-node which has just been activated is therefore received by the server. A worker task is allocated which attempts to locally activate the i-node, this task is held by the local i-node manager task, as the i-node is locked by the first worker. An apparent deadlock has occurred, however this is cured by the behaviour of the client. In the circumstances outlined above a reply to the first request will be received after sending the second, repeated, request. A further i-node operation will soon be performed to "release" or even "deactivate" the i-node. Once this has occurred the second worker task will gain access to the i-node and send a reply to the repeated "activate" request. Either this will fail because the client has already "put" the i-node, and therefore deallocated his reply Medium capability, or succeed, in which case the client receives a reply containing a capability to a fresh i-node request Medium. The client receives this reply when expecting the reply to some later transaction, therefore discards it and deallocates the enclosed Medium capability. This causes an exception to be raised in the second worker task as it was waiting for a request from a Medium which had no writers. In either case the second worker now tidies up and returns to the manager for more work.

The above scenario assumes no further message loss nor timeout occurs, however the argument still holds. The client's technique of discarding unwanted replies, and hence Medium capabilities, and the eventual deallocation of the i-node request and reply Mediums, guarantees that the server can recover, without tying up resources. This is true even in the face of a client crash, providing the kernel performs the correct action of deallocating outstanding capabilities to the client machine.

7.6.4 Directories

The package **naming** provides the uppermost layer within the implementation of files. The most important subprogram is **namei**, which converts a pathname string to an active i-node pointer. **Namei** repeatedly searches directories looking for a match with successive pathname components. It performs a similar function to its namesake within the UNIX kernel, the main difference being that notice is taken of whether the caller requires access for update or not. For file creation or deletion, for instance, the parent directory must be accessed for update. Hence whilst resolving the pathname, look-ahead is required to check whether the current component is the last or next to last.

It is worth considering what happens when a request to create a file within the working directory is received, when that working directory is a local duplicate copy. In this situation the working, or current, directory must be accessed for update, even though it was originally accessed for reading only. The situation is handled naturally by the fact that **namei** always explicitly re-activates the working directory at the beginning of a relative pathname search. Therefore the master copy's i-node is accessed for the update, even though the duplicate remains stored as the working directory. Moreover, the next reference for reading to the working directory will cause the local duplicate copy to be synchronised.

Since replication and remote file access are provided at a lower level, **namei** need not be concerned with such issues. When searching a directory for a given pathname component, for example, its does not know or care whether the directory file is local or remote, master or duplicate. It just calls on a subprogram within the **inode** package to return the directory's contents a disk block at a time. An alternative scheme would have made the addition, deletion and searching for directory entries, primitives supported by the private interface. This would have increased performance and provided more security, in that each file server would have more responsibility for its file store's integrity, at the expense of extra code and a more complex interface.

7.7 Statistics

In this section we give some indication of the size of the file server; performance figures are presented in the next chapter. All figures given are for a recent version of the file server constructed without any tracing code (which, if present, may be selectively switched on at run-time to aid debugging individual packages).

The file server comprises 46 packages, of which 12 contain only type declarations and 4 have bodies written in C, and a small main subprogram. The source of each package specification and each package body is stored in separate

UNIX files. In total there are 7,313 lines of Ada and 35 lines of C (including comments).

The object code generated comprises:

    14,656 bytes resident code,
    39,344 bytes overlaid code,
    4,278 bytes uninitialised data,
    and 304 bytes initialised data.

At run-time the PULSE kernel maps the file server code and data into 8 LSI-11 memory management segments, each of maximum size 8k bytes. The resident code occupies two segments, the overlaid code a single segment, two segments are reserved for stack space, and the other three segments are used for the data and heap. The data sizes given above are small since they refer to static storage. However, most of the space required by the file server is allocated from the heap dynamically, for example that needed for disk cache buffers and message space.

Once the file server has been through its initialisation phase, which includes creating all worker tasks and allocating data structures on the heap, its physical memory image currently takes up 108,864 bytes (this is larger than the 64k virtual address space of a user-level program due to the overlays and the per task system data areas, and depends upon how many clients, open files, disk buffers etc. are catered for). The total number of tasks in the file server is about 20.

7.8 Summary

The file server achieves its aims of providing a UNIX-like file service, incorporating both replication and distribution. Moreover it is completely written in Ada, save for a few small subprograms written in C, and makes extensive use of Ada tasking facilities. Many "bells and whistles" that are needed in a "real" system have been left unimplemented, partly for lack of code space. The number of resources provided, in terms of concurrent clients and open files, is also somewhat "unrealistic".

8 PERFORMANCE EVALUATION

8.1 Performance Evaluation of the PULSE Kernel

In this section we present and discuss the basic performance figures for the prototype kernel.

8.1.1 Rendezvous Times

operation	time in milliseconds	
	UNIX	PULSE
simple rendezvous	2.55	5.42
2 arm select no delay	3.05	6.79
3 arm select no delay	3.25	7.40
4 arm select no delay	3.45	7.99
2 arm select with delay	3.40	7.28
3 arm select with delay	3.60	7.91
4 arm select with delay	3.80	8.53

Table 8.1: Rendezvous Times

In the York Ada[79] implementation, where tasks are multiplexed within a single UNIX process, the average time taken for a simple rendezvous (no selection) is approximately 2.6 milliseconds on a LSI-11/23. The average time for a simple rendezvous on the same machine running the PULSE kernel is 5.4 milliseconds. Some of the difference is explained by the overhead of context switching between the

LSI-11/23 user and kernel mode which is about 0.5 of a millisecond. As explained in chapter 6 a simple rendezvous requires three traps into the system to handle the support routines "accept", "endaccept" and "enter". These will add at least another 1.5 milliseconds, the rest of the time is the overhead in maintaining more that one Ada program.

To select between two entries increases the average time of a rendezvous to 6.8 milliseconds (cf 3.1 milliseconds on UNIX); most of the increase is due to the two extra traps into the kernel to "post the accepts". For every extra arm in the select, the time increases by about 0.6 of a millisecond (cf 0.20 milliseconds on UNIX) to reflect the extra call into the kernel and increased processing. If one arm of the select is a delay statement then the time increases by 0.5 of a millisecond (cf 0.35 milliseconds on UNIX) to reflect the manipulation of the task into delay queues associated with the clock.

It is difficult to take measurements of the time for both an else clause in the select or conditional and timed entry calls due to the scheduling of the test programs. The time taken for an else clause in a select which is always executed is dominated by the number of traps into the kernel to post the accepts and to call the select routine. For timed entry calls the times are the same as for normal entry calls because the accepting task is always ready to accept. No rescheduling is done after the completion of the rendezvous, so the accepting task cycles around and is blocked at the next rendezvous before the calling task has had time to issue the call. This also applies to conditional entry calls.

8.1.2 Overlay Times

The average time taken to set up or restore an overlay is about 0.9 of a millisecond.

8.1.3 Allocating and Deallocating Mediums

The cost of allocating and deallocating a Medium is about 1.5 milliseconds.

8.1.4 Basic Communication Overhead

The PULSE IPC is built on top of the Ada rendezvous. The time taken for a user program to send a local null message and receive a local null reply, on an otherwise idle machine, is 18.4 milliseconds. For a remote send and a remote receive, on idle machines, the time is 40 milliseconds. These figures represent the basic communication overheads. The latter can be compared with the figures obtained by the Cambridge File Server (CFS) and the Xerox Distributed File Server (XDFS)[78].

System	Processor type and speed in MIPS millions of instructions per second	Communication Subsystem and point to point data bandwidth	Communication Overheads per transaction in milliseconds
CFS	CA LSI4/30 1Mip	Cambridge Ring 1Mbit/sec.	12ms
XDFS	ALTO 0.25Mips	Ethernet 2.82Mbits/sec	38ms
PULSE	LSI/11-23 0.2Mips	Cambridge Ring 1Mbit/sec	40ms

Table 8.2: Comparison of Communication Overheads

The time taken for data to be transmitted physically on the communication subsystem is small compared to the time spent preparing and processing the data. For example, the time taken for a minipacket to make a full circle of the Cambridge Ring is of the order of one instruction cycle on the LSI-11/23. The speed of data transfer is therefore dominated by the amount of processing performed and the native speed of the processor involved, rather than the data rate of the communication subsystem. In the case of the PULSE kernel, a Basic Block transaction is performed under program interrupt control. The speed of minipacket transfer is such that little else may be expected to happen during receipt or transmission apart from the processing of interrupts. The CFS also uses the Basic Block Protocol, whereas the XDFS uses the more expensive Pup protocol[11] which was designed for wide area as well as local area networks.

Given that the performance is dominated by the raw processing speed of the processors involved, the communication overheads are comparable with those obtained by Cambridge and Xerox.

8.1.5 Data Transaction Performance Figures

The PULSE IPC allows variable length messages, up to a maximum, to be sent. Currently the maximum size message is that required by the file system to send a disk block and some associated data (568 bytes). The average time taken for data transactions of variable sizes is now displayed. (A data transaction is one message with the data plus one null message acknowledging its receipt.) The time taken for 1000 transactions was measured and divided by 1000 to give the time taken for a single transaction. This was repeated 5 times and the average time per transaction was calculated. In all cases the data is of "unsafe data" type and the time excludes the time taken to set up the connection.

Two sets of figures are presented for transaction sizes ranging from 0 to 500 bytes. The first figure is for a transaction on the same machine and the second is for a transaction across the network.

Transaction size in bytes	Transaction time in milliseconds	
	local	remote
0	19.80 $\pm$ 0.02	40.00 $\pm$ 0.02
100	21.87 $\pm$ 0.01	60.00 $\pm$ 0.02
200	23.35 $\pm$ 0.03	80.01 $\pm$ 0.01
300	24.88 $\pm$ 0.02	100.00 $\pm$ 0.02
400	26.40 $\pm$ 0.02	120.01 $\pm$ 0.01
500	27.93 $\pm$ 0.03	140.00 $\pm$ 0.01

Table 8.3: Transaction Times With a Maintained Connection

From these figures the time taken to send a local transaction is given approximately by the formula:

LT = 20.35 + (0.0151*transaction size) $\pm$ 0.03 milliseconds
where 0 < size <= 512 bytes

Notice that the time taken for a zero byte transaction is slightly less than 20.3 milliseconds. This is due to an optimisation in the PULSE kernel for zero length unsafe data.

The time taken for a remote transaction is approximately given by the formula:

RT = 40.00 + (0.20 * transaction size) $\pm$ milliseconds
where 0 <= size <= 512 bytes

For remote transaction the kernel optimisation is small compared to the overall transaction time so the boundary conditions, for the formula, include zero.

In all cases the communication overhead associated with the transaction is significant to the overall transaction time; consequently it is much cheaper to send one large message than several smaller ones. For remote transactions the cost varies from 2 to 5 times the cost for a local transaction.

Comparison with the V Distributed Kernel

The time taken for a 512 byte data remote transaction is approximately 140 milliseconds. The time taken for a 0 byte remote transaction is approximately 40 milliseconds. This implies that the time taken to transfer 512 bytes of data from a task on one machine to a task on another is about 100 milliseconds (ignoring the overhead of setting up the basic block protocol). The time taken for a local transaction of 512 bytes is about 28 milliseconds whereas the time taken for a 0 byte local transaction is about 20 milliseconds. This implies the time taken to transfer 512 bytes into and out of the kernel is 8 milliseconds. The time taken, therefore, to transfer 512 bytes from the kernel of one machine to the kernel of another is about 92 milliseconds. This may be compared with 3 milliseconds, the time taken for the V kernel[18] to transfer data between two 10 MHz Sun work stations connected by a 3 Mbits Ethernet[76]. The LSI-11/23 is a 3.3 MHz processor, so clearly some of the difference can be accounted for in the difference in processor speeds; however, there is still a large performance difference.

In order to explain this difference the interfaces to the Cambridge Ring and to the Ethernet must be compared. The Cambridge Ring has a fixed packet size of two bytes whereas the Ethernet has variable size packets. Cheriton[18] gives the time taken to copy the data from the kernel to the Ethernet interface to be of the order of 1 millisecond. In the PULSE kernel prototype implementation, the time taken for the data to transferred to the Cambridge Ring interface is the time taken to handle 256 Cambridge Ring interrupts. To handle one Cambridge Ring interrupt takes the order of 50 LSI-11/23 instructions of an average 5 microseconds per instruction, giving a total time of about 0.25 milliseconds per interrupt. (In practice, as there are many register manipulation instructions, the average instruction time may well be as low as 4 microseconds, giving 0.2 milliseconds per interrupt.) The time taken to service 256 interrupts is between 51 and 64 milliseconds; similarly for a receive interrupt. Furthermore, the current implementation does not use the hardware retry facilities but does software retries when the destination node is busy. On average when sending a basic block the sender sends a minipacket before the receiver has processed the previous one. This results in a software retry which is handled at interrupt level. Consequently for a 512 byte basic block (256 words) 512 ring interrupts can be expected. The number of instructions to service an interrupt which indicates that the destination node was busy, and to retry, is about 40, giving an interrupt service time of between 0.16 and 0.2 microseconds. The time taken to handle the retry interrupts is therefore between 41 and 51 milliseconds. This second interrupt will overlap with the receive interrupt, giving a total time of between 92 and 115 milliseconds.

The difference in the performance of the V kernel and the PULSE kernel can be explained by the inefficient low level handling of the basic block protocol. There are two possible optimisations which can help improve the PULSE kernel's performance.

1) Allow the hardware to retry the transmission of a packet if the destination node is busy.

   A timeout must then be associated with the basic block as a whole.

2) Accept that while ring traffic is being handled no other processing is possible because of the raw speed of the device.

Once a basic block has commenced both machines should busy wait for the device and not be interrupt driven.

Even with either of these optimisations, the expected transfer time will still be significantly more than that experienced using an Ethernet.

This brief comparison of the Cambridge Ring and Ethernet fails to demonstrate that the Ring performs better under heavier loads and is more suitable for communication between processors of mismatched speeds. A more detailed performance evaluation has been done at Strathclyde University[9] using a simulation model.

For a Network Server outside the kernel, an increase by a factor of approximately 1.5 to 2.0 can be measured over a kernel based Network Server. This compares with a factor 4 measured in the V kernel[18]. However, these times are dominated by the problems of handling ring interrupts mentioned above.

Transaction Times Without a Maintained Connection

The figures presented, in the previous subsection, were for data transfer only; the connection time was not included. In this section the time taken to receive a message and send a reply is presented, where the write capability for the reply is sent with the message.

Transaction size in bytes	Transaction time in milliseconds	
	local	remote
0	25.23 ± 0.05	59.98 ± 0.04
100	27.24 ± 0.06	79.98 ± 0.04
200	28.76 ± 0.04	100.00 ± 0.02
300	30.29 ± 0.01	120.00 ± 0.02
400	31.79 ± 0.01	139.98 ± 0.02
500	33.27 ± 0.03	160.00 ± 0.02

Table 8.4: Transaction Times Without a Maintained Connection

It can be seen that for local transactions the cost of setting up the reply connection is approximately 5 in 25 milliseconds. (The cost of allocating a Medium and deallocating a Medium is about 1.5 milliseconds each.) For transactions which require many messages 25% of the time can be saved by maintaining the connection.

For remote transactions the figures are again dominated by the poor performance of the low level ring handling, so for 512 byte transactions only approximately 12.5% performance improvement can be expected by maintaining the transaction.

8.2 Distributed File System

Performance measurements of a program as complex as the PULSE file server are difficult to make and to interpret. We have attempted to measure its performance by timing certain common operations under various "file_map" settings with different situations regarding duplicate files (i.e. whether or not they exist, and if so whether they are up-to-date).

Measurements were taken on two LSI-11/23s running the same version of PULSE; one machine (local in the figures) uses an RP02 compatible CDC CMD style disk drive with average access time of 40 milliseconds per block, the other (remote) machine uses an RL02 compatible Winchester disk drive with average access time of 70 milliseconds. Both machines were idle apart from the execution of the test program on the local machine. We have not attempted to measure the file servers performance when responding to several concurrent requests, either locally or remotely.

The test program utilises the standard **fs_interface** package to send requests to the file server. This package provides a UNIX-like subprogram interface to the file server. Measurements were made by making calls on a kernel diagnostic routine before and after calls on **fs_interface**. Measurements thus include the overheads introduced by **fs_interface**. For example, to enable subprograms in this package to be called re-entrantly by more than one task in a user program, message space and a reply Medium capability are allocated and deallocated during each subprogram call.

8.2.1 File server operations

The file server operations measured were as follows:

stat   a "stat" operation is performed on an file in the current directory

cd   a "cd" i.e. change working directory operation is performed, moving the working directory a single level down the file hierarchy.

open/close   a file in the current directory is opened then immediately closed

read   one disk block (512 bytes) is read from an open file (average taken from reading fifty blocks sequentially)

write   one disk block (512 bytes) is written to an empty file (average taken from writing fifty blocks sequentially to a freshly created file)

set result   "set result" is the simplest file server operation - just causing the file server to store 1 word (16 bits) of information, which it later passes as an exit status to the client's parent program upon its termination. It is included purely to show the basic overhead in any request made to the file server.

In Tables 8.5 and 8.6, each column represents a particular sequence of actions taken by the file server, determined by the file_map setting and the existence of the various copies of the file in question. The particular file classes attempted are indicated as follows:

      lm - local master
      ld - local duplicate
      rm - remote master

Remote duplicate access is not yet supported.

An '*' placed next to a file class designates the particular file copy chosen. A further '*' signifies that the chosen duplicate file was also synchronised. This measurement will vary depending upon the size of the particular file. The actual size of file used was 512 bytes (1 disk block) for the "cd" and "stat" operations and 25k bytes (50 disk blocks) for the "open" operation. An unadorned file class indicates that file copy was looked for but did not exist. A '+' denotes a remote master file copy which was looked for, existed, but was not chosen.

The file server always attempts to access files in the order local master, local duplicate, remote master. For example in the first column the actual setting of the file_map for classes local duplicate and remote master are irrelevant since they are not considered once the local master is found.

The empty table entries correspond to invalid operations i.e. writing to a duplicate file.

8.2.2 General Measurements

Table 8.5 gives measurements of elapsed real time. Any single timing of a PULSE operation is only accurate to within 2 clock ticks, or 40 milliseconds. Short operations must therefore be repeated many times to give a measurement accurate to the nearest millisecond. Unfortunately this causes the effect of caching to come into play. Hence in all figures given, no physical disk I/O is performed except for the cases of reading and writing, moreover the work done to establish an initial connection with a remote file server is not included.

Distributed File System

Table 8.6 shows the number of traps into the kernel for overlay segment switches and the total number of traps into the kernel which includes task creation, rendezvous administration etc, Medium allocation and deallocation and message sending etc. and overlay segment switching. These counts are purely for the local machine activity and hence do not include the processing done on the remote machine, they do include however, traps into the kernel made by both the user (or "client") program and the file server itself.

Operation	Time in milliseconds					
	1m *	1d *	1m 1d *	1m 1d * rm +	1m 1d ** rm +	rm *
stat	61	61	67	439	511	401
cd	65	65	70	458	544	426
open/close	97	108	113	526	13600	536
read	68	68	68	68	68	222
write	116	-	-	-	-	288
set result	32	32	32	32	32	32

Table 8.5: File Server Operation Times

Operation	Overlay Traps / Total Traps					
	lm *	lm ld *	lm ld * rm +	lm ld * rm +	lm ld ** rm +	rm *
stat	16/23	16/23	20/27	28/49	28/51	22/39
cd	22/29	22/29	26/33	34/55	34/57	30/51
open/close	20/39	24/43	28/47	254/880	30/66	30/66
read	4/12	4/12	4/12	4/12	4/12	6/15
write	6/23	-	-	-	-	6/16
set result	0/7	0/7	0/7	0/7	0/7	0/7

Table 8.6: Kernel Traps for File Server Operations

8.2.3 Interpretation of Measurements

Local Access

The times for local access are very slow compared with UNIX running on the same machine. For example, it takes UNIX on average only 17 milliseconds of elapsed time to read a disk block from a large file. This may be explained by many factors: the file server is an independently scheduled program containing many tasks, message passing requires extra copying of data between address spaces, Ada code is generally slower than the equivalent C code, an Ada rendezvous takes a long time, the file server does not perform disk read ahead for local file access, etc. In particular, the number of traps into the kernel simply to perform overlay segment switches is considerable for all but the simplest file server operation.

The minimum number of traps into the kernel when performing any file server operation is given by the figure for "set_result" i.e. seven. These may be accounted for as follows. The user program allocates a reply Medium, sends the request message, receives the reply message and finally deallocates its reply Medium capability. The file server receives the request message, sends a reply, and deallocates its reply Medium capability.

Remote Access

A "stat" of a remote file or "cd" to a remote working directory takes over six times as long as the equivalent local operation. Reading or writing a remote file takes roughly three times as long as local file access. The smaller overhead in remote access for reading compared with a "stat" is due to the fact that only a single message is sent between machines in each direction in order to read a disk block from an open file, whereas several messages are involved upon initial file reference. One reason for this is that directory searching is performed on the local machine, by reading the directory remotely a block at a time. Another is that each remote file reference involves setting up a two way Medium connection between file servers, but that subsequent operations on the active file require no Medium capability transfers.

Even allowing for the number of messages sent between the machines, the increase in time for remote compared with local access (itself slow) is considerable. This is due to the overheads involved in message traffic across the ring. (see Table 8.3).

Replication

Costs due to replication are incurred solely at the initial file reference time, i.e. there are no costs when reading a duplicate file, only when opening or "stat"ing etc. The overheads on accessing a local duplicate file are negligible compared to that of local master: the extra disk access potentially required to read the i-map being avoided by the disk cache. A failed attempt to reference a local master copy prior to referencing a local duplicate incurs some cost, but little compared to that incurred by any remote access.

The time taken to check whether a duplicate file is up-to-date is considerable compared to simple local reference time, though not intolerable. If such a check results in a local duplicate copy being opened, then the cost of the check is soon offset when data is read. This is important since the time taken to read files is most likely to dominate the overall user-perceived performance of the PULSE distributed file system.

Perhaps the most interesting figures are those for referencing a duplicate file which is out of date and hence automatically synchronised. Obviously the larger the file, the larger the delay in the open time. The time to synchronise a 50 block file (13.6 seconds) is about half that of the sum of the times to read a 50 block file remotely and write a 50 block file locally (25.5 seconds), i.e. perform a user level file copy. This is purely because the synchronising is done directly by the file servers and does not invoke the overheads of context switching and message copying between file server and user program.

8.2.4 Nassi-Habermann Optimisation

The so called "Nassi-Habermann optimisation"[37] is a technique whereby an Ada implementation may avoid task switches for rendezvous with certain classes of "passive" tasks. This is achieved by executing the rendezvous code without the usual context switch from the calling task to the accepting task. It has not yet, to our knowledge, been implemented in any Ada compiler, since it is a severe problem to determine automatically whether a particular task is a suitable candidate for the optimisation.

In order to improve the file server's performance and to discover the usefulness of such an optimisation, the effect of the Nassi-Habermann optimisation was produced by writing the equivalent code "by hand". This was done for two tasks, the buffer manager task and the in-core i-node manager tasks, both of which are used extensively in most file server operations. The measurements presented in tables 8.5 and 8.6 above were produced from a file server with the optimisation. To show the benefits it gives, table 8.7 repeats the measurements for the simple case of local master file access, but also gives the measurements for the file server without the optimisation and an indication of the number of extra rendezvous incurred.

Operation	time in milliseconds		
	with NH	no NH	rendezvous saved
stat	61	111	6
cd	65	132	8
open/close	97	164	8
read	68	115	6
write	116	194	9
set result	32	32	0

Table 8.7: Effect of Nassi-Habermann Optimisation

Table 8.7 shows the implications of the high cost of the rendezvous, about 8 milliseconds each. The performance gains achieved by optimising away the rendezvous are typically between 50 and 100 per cent, depending upon the file server operation.

8.3 Summary

We have shown that overall performance of PULSE is disappointing. For local operations times are dominated by the message traffic between programs and by the overheads of the rendezvous. Hand-coded Nassi-Habermann optimisations have helped reduce the latter but more sympathetic hardware is required to alleviate the former. For remote operation, time is again dominated by the message traffic. The current implementation of the PULSE kernel fails to exploit fully the availability of a fast local area network due to the interrupt driven nature of the Cambridge Ring Interface. It is clear that significant improvements on remote transaction times, for an otherwise idle machine, can be achieved by changing to a non-interrupt driven driver. For example, experiments have indicated that the time taken for a transaction of 500 bytes with a maintained connection can be reduced from 140 milliseconds to 60 milliseconds. For heavier loads a Direct Memory Access (DMA) device would be necessary to maintain that improvement. At present, such devices are not available for the LSI-11/23.

We have measured the performance of the PULSE file server for certain common operations under differing "file map" settings. The overheads introduced by replication and distribution are low enough to give a reasonable degree of "performance transparency"[103] in the file server's provision of "network transparency". Given more efficient message passing (both local and remote), we suggest that a similar if not better degree of performance transparency could be achieved even if local file access time were greatly reduced.

A fundamental performance problem caused by the file system architecture is the need to check whether a local duplicate file copy is up-to-date before referencing it. In a lightly loaded system this overhead has been shown to be acceptable. In a "real" environment, however, this might not be the case, due to concurrent access to the same files. Directory searching is most likely to suffer, since many users will replicate the same directories at the top of the global tree, causing a potential bottleneck. In this situation the user may use the file selection control ("file_map") to eliminate references to remote master files for most of his work. His files may still be brought up-to-date by running the file synchronisation utility in background. Since directories are relatively stable, an extension to the file control mechanism could allow it to be specified for directories and files independently. This would allow the user to be guaranteed access to the latest version of duplicated data files, without overheads being incurred during directory searching. To give finer control we could allow the user to specify a interval during which an "up-to-date" check for a particular file would not be repeated.

9 RETROSPECTIVE

In this final chapter we look back over what we have and have not done, what we might have done, and what we should have done. The work presented in this book has been carried out over the last 5 years. During the first six months two fundamental design decisions were made which have greatly influenced the direction the research has taken. The first was that the general architecture of our distributed system should be based on a network of personal computers where machines are equally viable connected to, or disconnected from, the network. The second was that the system should be implemented in Ada and should support the development, testing and maintenance of Ada programs.

9.1 General Architecture

The characteristics of a network of personal computers have constrained the overall system architecture. Some issues have been simplified; for example, support is not provided directly for program execution on a processor other than a user's personal computer; hence the question of load balancing does not arise. On the other hand, we have had to look at the problems caused by allowing users to connect and disconnect freely to and from the network.

The personal computer model assumes that both processing power and disk storage are not in short supply. Hence the purpose of our distributed operating system is to make the sharing of resources easy, rather than making the optimal usage of them. To this end our efforts have concentrated on the provision of a distributed file system. Its design strives for simplicity in co-ordinating the individual file stores, each of which must be accessible when running stand-alone.

We have no doubts that the ability to name a file by a single absolute pathname (links excepted) from any part of the network, when combined with the ability to access files in a network transparent manner, provides a distributed system that is natural and easy to use. For example, having once used PULSE it can be irritating to return to an environment in which files must be explicitly moved from machine to machine, using a special program (in our case uucp) with a user-visible machine naming convention.

When using PULSE, we have noted the particular ease with which one can move one's working directory across machine boundaries without causing any confusion. The shell's pathname searches for executable programs may also cross machine boundaries, but the fact that any located program always executes on the user's own processor seems natural. There are times when it is possible to forget about the existence of the network completely. For example, occasionally a file has been referenced (typically to execute a program) without the user realising it was remote, the truth becoming apparent only when later running stand-alone. A more sophisticated automatic replication scheme would, of course, avoid this confusion! (At present a user chooses explicitly whether or not a file is to be replicated. It is not felt reasonable for the system to decide to replicate an arbitrary referenced remote file, since it may be very large or of no further interest.)

We maintain unique absolute pathnames for files by means of our primary copy replication scheme. Adopted slavishly, this causes problems in the case of temporary files. If we imagine the pathname of a directory in which user programs may expect to create temporary files, e.g. /usr/tmp, then all such files must, by the rules of our replication scheme, be created on the single machine which contains the master copy of that directory. This is clearly impractical, and in fact we must relax our rules to allow a special class of duplicate file to be independently updated. Such a directory file may have files created within it locally without reference to its master copy. Essentially, it is a file to which "multiple copy updates" are allowed yet never synchronised. It may be used as a globally known directory for the creation of temporary files. Although we cannot prevent such files being created with the same absolute pathnames, no confusion or conflict should arise due to their transient nature.

There are several paths of research which we have not had time to follow. We simplified matters by assuming a "friendly" environment and hence have not investigated novel protection schemes. We have not attempted to extend the UNIX model of a file system to incorporate support for atomic (recoverable) transactions (particularly desirable in a distributed system).

The small size of our network has hindered the development of some features. In particular we have been unable to experiment with sophisticated crash recovery schemes such as automatically switching file access between remote machines, nor to test fully the practicality of our simple broadcasting scheme for locating remote files. A larger number of machines in our network would also have demonstrated more convincingly the benefits to be gained from our file replication scheme, as well as pointing out any unforeseen problems.

9.2 Using Ada

The decision to use Ada has proved to be controversial both within and without the project. The use of Ada has had three particular drawbacks.

1) Reliance on the York Ada Compiler Project

    When we originally started the project there were no Ada compilers available let alone a validated one. The compiler project started at approximately the same time so from the outset we have always depended on it. We underestimated, as did they (and most other compiler groups), the amount of effort that would be required to produce a compiler. The continuously changing language during the period from the original Green language to the "final" ANSI standard has taken its toll.

    Whilst, to some extent, we have been able to drive the compiler project in that the facilities we have required have been given priority where possible, we have always been working with a subset of the language. For example, we have not been able to make use of generics or derived types; also private types were not available during our major implementation phase.

Further problems have been caused by the relatively unsophisticated code generation scheme used by the present York compiler. In particular we have the need for more efficient code when dealing with packages. Under the current scheme if one procedure or function is referenced in a package then all the code for that package is included. This conflicts with the grouping together of related routines into a single package. For example we have a single package which contains the message passing interfaces into the file system. These routine provided operations for opening, closing, linking etc. of files. The code size for the package is large (10K bytes); unfortunately any program which references a single procedure will result in all the package being included.

We have also found problems with the lack of any global optimisation techniques. In particular, unnecessary checks for null pointers are expensive both in code size and in execution time. We have been forced to turn off all such checks; if we had global flow optimisation then we perhaps could live with their cost.

One of the features of our design is that we have relied heavily upon Ada tasking. Fairly early on it was realised that sophisticated optimisation techniques are required if task communication is to be efficient. One can only speculate as to whether techniques such as the Nassi-Habermann optimisation[37] are likely to be put into practice by Ada compiler writers. Although we tried not to rely on such techniques, ultimately we resorted to hand-coded optimisations to improve performance.

Finally, there have been very few tools available for debugging Ada programs, particularly in a stand-alone environment. Although a significant amount of debugging of the file server was done under UNIX using "sdb", when running stand-alone we had to resort to "print" statements and sometimes to studying the machine code generated.

2) Using an Untried Language

Although Ada was designed from a set of language requirements which were meant to be attainable within the state of the art it was a new language which was untried. When we started our project there was no experience in using the language, there were no books on how to program in Ada, no portability or style guides and no caveats concerning its use. To a large extent we have been on our own; we have had to develop our own techniques and have made mistakes which could have been avoided given a well understood, less complex, language. We have found problems in the language which have not been documented. These problems have caused us further delays and have sometimes forced us to concentrate on Ada issues rather than issues of distribution.

3) No Host Compiler for the LSI-11/23

Unfortunately we do not have a host compiler for the LSI-11/23 (if such a thing is possible), consequently all our development is on a VAX using a cross compiler and requires transferring code onto the LSI-11 for testing. As well as complicating debugging, this has meant that our prototype PULSE system is not self-supporting, an attribute which would undoubtedly have aided the production of a realistic, reliable system.

Also the small address space, both virtual and physical, of the LSI-11/23 has proved incompatible with the general verbosity of code produced by Ada. We were forced to introduce an overlay facility for the file server programs; in addition to increasing execution time, this has made debugging more complicated.

These three points illustrate the cost to the project of using Ada. If we view the project purely as a program of research in distributed operating systems then clearly this cost has been significant and many months of effort have been wasted; it has also resulted in the project being relatively conservative in its distributed system design. However, we have investigated the use of Ada in a distributed environment and have also discovered significant problems when Ada is used for resource allocation. (These are discussed in appendix C.)

Among the positive features of the use of Ada, we have found packages and secure separate compilation to be invaluable for programming a (relatively) large piece of software.

9.3 Distributed Programming

The decision to use Ada led to our investigation of how independent Ada programs should communicate in a distributed system, which in turn led to the design of the Medium concept. Much of our experience in using Mediums has come from the file server, which is by far the most complex "distributed program" which we have written. The few, simple operations which may be performed with Mediums certainly aid the writing and understanding of such a program (many message-based systems have a complex interface with several different ways of doing the same thing, for example the Accent[89] system from which we adopted some ideas). On the other hand, this simplicity can cause inefficiency, such as the need to create several tasks to overcome the inability to wait for a message from one of several Mediums at the same time. For example, the file server must assign a task to each open file Medium, thereby restricting the total number of open files possible due to the memory overheads of tasks.

The kernel run-time checking of message types has proved of limited value in detecting programming errors (it is clearly of limited generality), although it has enabled the file server to avoid the use of unsafe conversion when constructing and decoding messages. The use of a strong type checking language together with the kernel protection of Medium capabilities has proved to be enough to make the uncontrolled sending of messages to arbitrary Mediums most unlikely. A more common cause of error has been that of a program sending a message using an out-of-date, rather than incorrect, message structure. The kernel provides no support to detect this occurrence.

9.4 Closing Remarks

A network of powerful personal computers, linked by a high-speed local area network, is being seen increasingly as an alternative to a traditional centralised time-sharing operating system. We have shown that such a system may be constructed to give the benefits of a self-sufficient personal computer to each user whilst not losing the facilities for communication and sharing of data inherent in centralised systems.

Appendix A: THE ADA REPRESENTATION OF THE PULSE IPC

In this appendix we present the complete text of the package pulse_ipc. It forms the basis of the PULSE IPC and is used by most packages.

```
------------------------------------------------------
--                   PULSE_IPC                      --
------------------------------------------------------

with pulse_types; use pulse_types;
with fs_int_types; use fs_int_types;
with pstandard; use pstandard;
package pulse_ipc is

---------------------BASIC TYPES---------------------

   type medium_t;
   type medium is access medium_t;

   type a_byte_t is array(natural range<>) of byte_t;
   type a_integer is array(natural range<>) of integer;
   type a_float is array(natural range<>) of float;
   type a_boolean is array(natural range<>) of boolean;
   type a_transfer_t is array(natural range<>) of medium;

   BACKLOG :constant integer := 1;
   subtype backlog_of_messages_t is integer range 1..BACKLOG;

   type message_class_t is ( MEDIUM_DATA);
```

```
type data_class_t is ( BYTES, DISK_BLOCK,
     INTEGERS, CHARACTERS, REALS, BOOLEANS,
     READ_TRANSFERS, WRITE_TRANSFERS, ALL_TRANSFERS,
     BIO, UNSAFE, NEW_PROGRAM, LOAD_PROGRAM,
     FSR, OFR, FS_REPLY, OF_REPLY, PEXIT,
     RINO_REQUEST, RINO_REPLY,
     DATA_DESCS, NIL );


type rejection_t is (BREAK, PABORT);


type load_op_t is ( LOAD_TEXT, LOAD_DATA,
     START_PROGRAM, RAISE_EXCEPTION, READ_TEXT,
     READ_DATA, READ_STACK, NIL );


type bio_req_t is
   record
      base_addr     : p_disk_block_t;
      count         : integer;
      disk_adr      : disk_adr_t;
      minor_device  : minor_range_t;
      device_op     : integer;
   end record;


type unsafe_t is
   record
      count         : integer;
      adr           : address_t;
   end record;


type new_program_req_t is
   record
      text_size     : integer;
      data_size     : integer;
      entry_point   : address_t;
   end record;
```

```ada
type load_program_op_t(load_op: load_op_t := LOAD_DATA) is
  record
    case load_op is
      when LOAD_DATA =>
        seg_num               : integer;
        seg_data              : p_disk_block_t;
      when START_PROGRAM =>
        file_sys_medium       : medium;
        lifeline              : medium;
        exit_medium           : medium;
        priority              : priority_t;
      when RAISE_EXCEPTION =>
        name                  : rejection_t;
      when others =>
        null;
    end case;
  end record;
```

--------FILE SYSTEM REQUEST AND REPLY FORMATS------

```ada
type fsr_code_t is ( FSR_CLONE, FSR_EXECUTE,
     FSR_WAIT, FSR_NOWAIT, FSR_OPEN, FSR_CREATE,
     FSR_FSTAT, FSR_LINK, FSR_UNLINK, FSR_CHOWN,
     FSR_CHMOD, FSR_MAKE_NODE, FSR_CHDIR, FSR_PIPE,
     FSR_ACCESS_CHECK, FSR_SET_UID, FSR_GET_UID,
     FSR_MAKE_PRES, FSR_MAKE_ABS, FSR_SET_MAP,
     FSR_SET_RESULT );
```

```ada
type fs_request_t(request: fsr_code_t := FSR_OPEN) is
  record
      pathname         : unsafe_t;
      link_dup_path    : unsafe_t;
      case request is
        when FSR_OPEN =>
           open_mode : open_mode_t;
        when FSR_CREATE =>
           file_mode : file_mode_t;
        when FSR_WAIT | FSR_NOWAIT =>
           child     : pid_t;
        when FSR_CHOWN =>
           new_owner : owner_t;
        when FSR_CHMOD =>
           new_mode : file_mode_t;
        when FSR_ACCESS_CHECK =>
           check_mode : access_permission_t;
        when FSR_SET_UID =>
           uid : owner_t;
        when FSR_SET_MAP =>
           file_map : file_map_t;
        when FSR_SET_RESULT =>
           result_value : integer;
        when FSR_EXECUTE =>
           priority : priority_t;
        when others =>
           null;
      end case;
  end record;


type fsr_result_t is (
         SUCCESS,
         TOO_MANY_PROGS,    -- from load
         NO_CHILD,          -- from wait
         DEFUNCT,           -- child was still-born
         MISC_FAIL          -- miscellaneous failure
            );
```

```ada
type fs_reply_t(request :fsr_code_t := FSR_OPEN) is
   record
      result : fsr_result_t;
      case request is
         when FSR_PIPE =>
            in_end  : medium;
            out_end : medium;
         when FSR_FSTAT =>
            buffer : unsafe_t;
         when FSR_WAIT | FSR_NOWAIT =>
            exit_status : exit_status_t;
         when others =>
            null;
      end case;
   end record;


type of_request_code_t is (OF_READ, OF_WRITE,
                           OF_STAT, OF_IOCTL,
                           OF_ASSERT, OF_LOCATE, OF_SEEK);


type of_request_t (request :of_request_code_t:=OF_READ) is
   record
      buffer : unsafe_t;
      case request is
         when OF_READ =>
            byte_count      : integer;
         when OF_IOCTL =>
            ioctl_request   : integer;
         when OF_SEEK =>
            offset : offset_t;
            how    : seek_mode_t;
         when others =>
            null;
      end case;
   end record;


type of_reply_code_t is (OFR_OK, OFR_ACCESS,
                         OFR_IOERR, OFR_EOF);
```

```
type of_reply_t(request: of_request_code_t:= OF_READ) is
   record
      result : of_reply_code_t;
      buffer : unsafe_t;
      case request is
         when OF_WRITE =>
            byte_count : integer;
         when OF_SEEK =>
            offset : offset_t;
         when others =>
            null;
      end case;
   end record;


type exit_t is
   record
      k_pid : integer;
      kernel_result : integer;
   end record;

---------REMOTE INODE OPERATION FORMATS-------------

   type rino_request_code_t is ( RINO_LOCATE_VOL,
         RINO_GET, RINO_LOCK, RINO_RELEASE,
         RINO_PUT, RINO_READ, RINO_WRITE,
         RINO_ASSERT, RINO_LOCATE );

   type rino_reply_code_t is (-- only success/fail
         RINO_GOOD, RINO_BAD );

   type rino_request_t is record
      request_code : rino_request_code_t;
      gino         : global_inumber_t;  -- LOCATE_VOL, GET
      count        : integer;           -- READ
      offset       : offset_t;          -- READ, WRITE
      inode_data   : unsafe_t;          -- RELEASE, PUT
      write_data   : unsafe_t;          -- WRITE
   end record;
```

Ada Representation of the PULSE IPC

```ada
type rino_reply_t is record
    reply_code  : rino_reply_code_t;
    gino        : global_inumber_t;  -- LOCATE, GET
    volume      : real_vol_t;        -- LOCATE
    count       : integer;           -- WRITE
    inode_data  : unsafe_t;          -- GET, LOCK
    read_data   : unsafe_t;          -- READ
end record;


---------------ACCESS POINTER TYPES ---------------

type p_a_byte_t is access a_byte_t;
type p_a_integer is access a_integer;
type p_a_float is access a_float;
type p_a_boolean is access a_boolean;
type p_a_transfer_t is access a_transfer_t;
type p_bio_req_t is access bio_req_t;
type p_unsafe_t is access unsafe_t;
type p_new_program_req_t is access new_program_req_t;
type p_load_program_op_t is access load_program_op_t;
type p_fs_request_t is access fs_request_t;
type p_of_request_t is access of_request_t;
type p_fs_reply_t is access fs_reply_t;
type p_of_reply_t is access of_reply_t;
type p_rino_request_t is access rino_request_t;
type p_rino_reply_t is access rino_reply_t;
type a_data_desc_t;
type p_a_data_desc_t is access a_data_desc_t;
type p_exit_t is access exit_t;
```

------------------DATA DESCRIPTOR------------------

```
type data_desc_t(data_class :data_class_t:=BYTES) is
   record
      case data_class is
         when BYTES =>
            byte_data              : p_a_byte_t;
         when DISK_BLOCK =>
            block_data             : p_disk_block_t;
         when INTEGERS =>
            integer_data           : p_a_integer;
         when CHARACTERS =>
            string_data            : p_string;
         when REALS =>
            float_data             : p_a_float;
         when BOOLEANS =>
            boolean_data           : p_a_boolean;
         when READ_TRANSFERS =>
            read_transfer_data     : p_a_transfer_t;
         when WRITE_TRANSFERS =>
            write_transfer_data    : p_a_transfer_t;
         when ALL_TRANSFERS =>
            all_transfer_data      : p_a_transfer_t;
         when BIO =>
            bio_request_data       : p_bio_req_t;
         when UNSAFE =>
            unsafe_data            : p_unsafe_t;
         when NEW_PROGRAM =>
            new_prog_req_data      : p_new_program_req_t;
         when LOAD_PROGRAM =>
            load_prog_op_data      : p_load_program_op_t;
         when FSR =>
            fsr_data               : p_fs_request_t;
         when OFR =>
            ofr_data               : p_of_request_t;
         when FS_REPLY =>
            fs_reply_data          : p_fs_reply_t;
         when OF_REPLY =>
            of_reply_data          : p_of_reply_t;
         when PEXIT =>
            exit_data              : p_exit_t;
         when RINO_REQUEST =>
            rino_request_data      : p_rino_request_t;
         when RINO_REPLY =>
            rino_reply_data        : p_rino_reply_t;
```

```ada
            when DATA_DESCS =>
               dd_data                 : p_a_data_desc_t;
            when others =>
               null;
         end case;
      end record;

   type a_data_desc_t is array(natural range <>)
                             of data_desc_t;



-----------------ACTUAL MESSAGE STRUCTURE-----------------

   type message_t ( data_class : data_class_t := BYTES ) is
      record
         reply       :medium;
         transfer    :medium;
         my_ref      :integer;
         user_code   :integer;
         dd          :data_desc_t(data_class);
      end record;

   type p_message_t is access message_t;



--------------- MESSAGE SUBTYPES----------------------
   subtype byte_message_t is message_t(BYTES);
   subtype integer_message_t is message_t(INTEGERS);
   subtype disk_block_message_t is message_t(DISK_BLOCK);
   subtype character_message_t is message_t(CHARACTERS);
   subtype bio_message_t is message_t(BIO);
   subtype unsafe_message_t is message_t(UNSAFE);
   subtype new_program_message_t is message_t(NEW_PROGRAM);
   subtype load_program_message_t is message_t(LOAD_PROGRAM);
   subtype fsr_message_t is message_t(FSR);
   subtype ofr_message_t is message_t(OFR);
   subtype fs_reply_message_t is message_t(FS_REPLY);
   subtype of_reply_message_t is message_t(OF_REPLY);
   subtype rino_request_message_t is message_t(RINO_REQUEST);
   subtype rino_reply_message_t is message_t(RINO_REPLY);
   subtype data_desc_message_t is message_t(DATA_DESCS);
   subtype exit_message_t is message_t(PEXIT);
   subtype null_message_t is message_t(NIL);
```

-------------------MEDIUM DECLARATION------------------------

```
   task type medium_t is

      entry send_message(this_message:in p_message_t);
      entry receive_message(this_message:in out p_message_t);

   end medium_t;

   type capability_t is (WRITEC,READC, ALLC);

   pragma libname("MEDALLOC");
   function medalloc(backlog: backlog_of_messages_t)
                    return medium;

   pragma libname("MEDDEALLOC");
   procedure meddealloc(med: in out medium;
                        cap: in capability_t);

   pragma libname("ACCEPTREPLY");
   function acceptreply return medium;
end pulse_ipc;
```

Appendix B: PULSE PROGRAMMER'S MANUAL ENTRIES

In this appendix we give examples of the PULSE programmer's manual entries. There are three sections: the first contains examples of some of the standard tools which are available, the second contains the package specification of some of the standard packages and the third contains examples of the details of the proceedures in those packages (we include only those present in the package fs_int).

CP(1)   PULSE Programmer's Manual   CP(1)

NAME

    cp - copy files

SYNOPSIS

    cp file1 file2

    cp [-p] file ... directory

DESCRIPTION

File1 is copied onto _file2_. The mode and owner of _file2_ are preserved if it already existed; the mode of the source file is used otherwise.

In the second form, one or more _files_ are copied into the _directory_ with their original file-names. If the -p option is present then the files are copied in parallel.

_Cp_ refuses to copy a file onto itself.

BUGS

If two files with the same names are copied then either the first file copied will be overwritten by the second, or if the -p option is given then some arbitrary mixture of the two files will be produced.

LS(1)   PULSE Programmer's Manual   LS(1)

NAME

    ls - list contents of directory

SYNOPSIS

    ls [-lsi] name ...

DESCRIPTION

For each directory argument, _ls_ lists the contents of the directory; for each file argument, _ls_ repeats its name and any other information requested. When no argument is given, the current directory is listed. There are several options:

-l   List in long format, giving file class, file location, number of links, owner and size in bytes, for each file.

-s Give size in blocks, including indirect blocks, for each entry.

-i Print i-number in first column of the report for each file listed.

MAKE_DUP(1)   PULSE Programmer's Manual   MAKE_DUP(1)

NAME

    make_dup - make a duplicate file

SYNOPSIS

    make_dup name ...

DESCRIPTION

    Make_dup makes local duplicates of the files named. The file map setting must have local duplicate and remote master access enabled.

RM_DUP(1)   PULSE Programmer's Manual   RM_DUP(1)

NAME

    rm_dup - remove a local duplicate file

SYNOPSIS

    rm_dup name ..

DESCRIPTION

    Rm_dup removes local duplicates of the named files.

TOOLS(1)   PULSE Programmer's Manual   TOOLS(1)

NAME

    cat   - catenate and print

    cmp   - compare two files

    echo - echo arguments

    grep - search a file for a pattern

    ed   - text editor

    wc   - word count

SYNOPSIS

    cat [file] ..

    cmp file1 file2

    echo [arg] ..

    ed name

    grep expression file ..

    wc [file]

DESCRIPTION

    These are the standard software tools as described by Kernighan[60] written in Ada.

ARGS(2)　　　　　　　　PULSE Programmer's Manual　　　　　　　　ARGS(2)

NAME

args - manipulate arguments

SYNOPSIS

with pstandard; **use** pstandard;
with pulse_ipc; **use** pulse_ipc;
package args **is**

    function argc **return** integer;
    function argv(arg : integer) **return** p_string;
    function argcm **return** integer;
    function argvm(arg : integer) **return** medium;

end args;

DESCRIPTION

This package enables a program to manipulate its arguments. There are two type: character strings and Mediums. The number of character string arguments and the number of Medium arguments are returned by the function argc and argcm respectively. The function argv and argvm return a numbered argument.

BUGS

The character string arguments are numbered from 0 whereas the Medium arguments are numbered from 1.

FS_INTERFACE(2)   PULSE Programmer's Manual   FS_INTERFACE(2)

NAME

fs_interface - file system interface

SYNOPSIS

with fs_int_types, pstandard, pulse_ipc;
use fs_int_types, pstandard, pulse_ipc;
package fs_interface **is**

    type file_t **is private**;
    NO_FILE : **constant** file_t;

    function open(s:string; m:open_mode_t) **return** file_t;
    function creat(s:string;f:file_mode_t) **return** file_t;
    procedure close(file:**in out** file_t);

```
function read(file:file_t; b:integer; size:integer)
                    return integer;
function write(file:file_t; b:integer; size:integer)
                    return integer;
function seek (file:file_t;offset:long_int;
            whence:seek_mode_t) return long_int;
procedure assert(file: file_t; med : medium);
function locate(file: file_t) return medium;
function f_to_m(file : file_t) return medium;
function m_to_f(med : medium) return file_t;
function link(s1,s2:string) return boolean;
function unlink(s1:string) return boolean;
function chdir( s: string) return boolean;
function mknod(s:string; mode: file_mode_t)
                    return boolean;
function chmod(s:string; mode : file_mode_t)
                    return boolean;
function chown(s:string; owner : owner_t)
                    return boolean;
procedure stat(name: string;
            stbuf: in out stat_buf_t;
            ok  : out boolean)
procedure clone(new_fs: out medium;
                        pid: out integer);
function newfs( newmed: medium) return medium;
procedure exec(s : string; his_fs: medium;
            lifeline : out medium;
            pri : priority_t;
            succ : out boolean);
function wait( pid : integer) return exit_status_t;
procedure nowait( pid : integer);
procedure set_result(res : integer);
procedure set_map(file_map: file_map_t);
function make_dup(s: string) return boolean;
function rm_dup(s: string) return boolean;

private
    type file_t is
        record
            ofm : medium;       -- open file medium
        end record;

    NO_FILE : constant file_t := (ofm => null);

end;
```

DESCRIPTION

This package provides a UNIX-like file system interface to the PULSE File System along with some PULSE specific file system requests.

The individual routines are described in Section 3 of this manual.

BUGS

The private type <u>file t</u> should be derived from type <u>medium</u> rather than a record type - not yet supported by the compiler.

P_TEXT_IO(2)   PULSE Programmer's Manual   P_TEXT_IO(2)

NAME

p_text_io - pulse text_io

SYNOPSIS

```
with pstandard, fs_int_types, fs_interface;
use  pstandard, fs_int_types, fs_interface;
package p_text_io is
   type stream_t is private;
   STDIN   : constant stream_t;
   STDOUT  : constant stream_t;
   STDERR  : constant stream_t;
   NO_STREAM : constant stream_t;
   type stream_buffering_t is (BUF_ON,BUF_OFF);
   IO_ERROR : exception;


   function fopen(s : string; mode : open_mode_t)
                    return stream_t;
   function fopen(f : file_t; mode : open_mode_t)
                    return stream_t;
   procedure fclose(stream : stream_t);
   function fseek(stream : stream_t;
            offset : long_int; whence : seek_mode_t)
```

```
                        return long_int;
   procedure fflush(stream : stream_t);
   procedure setbuf(stream : stream_t;
             buffering : stream_buffering_t);
   procedure cleanup;

   procedure put( s : string );
   procedure put( stream :stream_t; s : string);
   procedure put_line( s : string );
   procedure put_line( stream : stream_t; s : string);
   procedure put( c : character);
   procedure put( stream : stream_t; c : character);
   procedure put_line(c: character);
   procedure put_line(stream:stream_t; c : character);
   procedure put( i : integer );
   procedure put( stream : stream_t; i : integer);
   procedure put_line( i : integer);
   procedure put_line( stream:stream_t; i : integer);

   procedure new_line;
   procedure new_line(stream : stream_t);

   procedure get( i    : out integer;
                  eof : out boolean );
   procedure get( stream : stream_t;
                  i     : out integer;
                  eof   : out boolean);
   procedure get( c    : out character;
                  eof : out boolean);
   procedure get( stream : stream_t;
                  c      : out character;
                  eof    : out boolean);
   procedure get_line(s   : out string;
                      pos : integer;
                      eof : out boolean;
                      size : out integer);
   procedure get_line(stream : stream_t;
                      s : out string;
                      pos : integer;
                      eof : out boolean;
                      size : out integer);

   procedure dup( file1 : stream_t; file2 : stream_t);
   function dup( stream : stream_t) return stream_t;

   function filen( stream : stream_t) return file_t;
```

```
    private
        type stream_t is range -1 .. integer'last;
        STDIN     : constant stream_t := 0;
        STDOUT    : constant stream_t := 1;
        STDERR    : constant stream_t := 2;
        NO_STREAM : constant stream_t := -1;
    end p_text_io;
```

DESCRIPTION

   This package provides the PULSE equivalent to UNIX standard I/O. Optionally buffered I/O streams are provided - by default streams are unbuffered.

   The overloaded procedures get and put provide string, character and integer I/O. The procedure cleanup is used to flush all the buffers and close all files. It must be explicitly called before program termination since the package itself cannot detect this condition.

ASSERT(3)   PULSE Programmer's Manual   ASSERT(3)

NAME

   assert - associate a medium with an open file

PACKAGE

   fs_int

SYNOPSIS

   procedure assert(file : file_t; med : medium)

DESCRIPTION

   Assert associates a medium with an open file (see also locate). File is an open file descriptor which has been returned by open.

   The caller must have opened the file for writing.

BUGS

Failure is never reported.

CHDIR(3)   PULSE Programmer's Manual   CHDIR(3)

NAME

chdir - change working directory

PACKAGE

fs_int

SYNOPSIS

function chdir(s : string) **return** boolean

DESCRIPTION

String s is the pathname of a directory. Chdir causes this directory to become the current working directory, i.e. the starting point for path names not beginning with '/'.

DIAGNOSTICS

TRUE is returned if the working directory is changed; FALSE is returned if the given name is not that of a directory or is not searchable.

CHMOD(3)   PULSE Programmer's Manual   CHMOD(3)

NAME

chmod - change mode of file

PACKAGE

fs_int

SYNOPSIS

function chmod(s : string; mode : file_mode_t) **return** boolean

DESCRIPTION

The file whose name is given by the string s has its mode changed to mode.

COMPONENT TYPES

In package - fs_int_types.

```
type file_type_t is ( FT_DIR,
    FT_CHARACTER_SPECIAL, FT_BLOCK_SPECIAL,
    FT_REGULAR );

type file_access_t is ( FA_READ,
    FA_WRITE, FA_EXECUTE );

type access_permission_t is array(file_access_t)
            of boolean;
type user_class_t is (UC_OWNER, UC_GROUP, UC_OTHERS);

type access_list_t is array(user_class_t)
            of access_permission_t;
type file_mode_t is record
    file_type : file_type_t;
    access_permissions : access_list_t;
end record;
```

DIAGNOSTIC

TRUE is returned if the mode is changed; FALSE is returned if **s** cannot be found.

BUGS

Should check invoker is owner of file or super-user.

CHOWN(3)   PULSE Programmer's Manual   CHOWN(3)

NAME

chown - change owner of a file

PACKAGE

fs_int

SYNOPSIS

function chown(s : string; owner : owner_t) **return** boolean

DESCRIPTION

The file whose name is given by string **s** has its **owner** changed as specified.

COMPONENT TYPES

In package - fs_int_types

```
subtype user_id_t is short_int;
subtype group_id_t is short_int;

SUPER_UID : constant user_id_t := 0;

type owner_t is record
    user    : user_id_t;
    group   : group_id_t;
end record;
```

DIAGNOSTICS

TRUE is returned if the owner is changed; FALSE is returned if the file does not exist.

BUGS

No checks on the user's identity are made.

CLONE(3)   PULSE Programmer's Manual   CLONE(3)

NAME

clone - create a new file system request medium

PACKAGE

fs_int

SYNOPSIS

procedure clone(new_fs : **out** medium; pid : **out** integer)

DESCRIPTION

Clone creates a new file system request medium with the same characteristics as the current file system request medium. This may be used as an alternative file system request medium (see newfs) or in the process of executing a new program (see exec).

Pid is the program identifier used to reference a possible subsequently executed program (see exec and wait).

CLOSE(3)   PULSE Programmer's Manual   CLOSE(3)

NAME

    close - close a file

PACKAGE

    fs_int

SYNOPSIS

    procedure close(fs : **in out** file_t)

DESCRIPTION

    Given an open file medium such as returned from an open or creat, close closes the associated file.

    Files are closed automatically on program termination via the file server detecting no writers to the open file mediums, but since there is a limit on the number of medium capabilities per program, close is necessary for programs which deal with many files.

CREAT(3)   PULSE Programmer's Manual   CREAT(3)

NAME

    creat - create a new file

PACKAGE

    fs_int

SYNOPSIS

    function creat(s : string; f : file_mode_t) **return** file_t

DESCRIPTION

   Creat creates a new file or prepares to rewrite an existing file called s.

   If the file did exist it is truncated to 0 length. The file is also opened for writing, and its open file descriptor is returned.

   The mode given is arbitrary; it need not allow writing.

COMPONENT TYPES

   In package - fs_int_types.

   type file_type_t **is** (FT_DIR, FT_CHARACTER_SPECIAL, FT_BLOCK_SPECIAL, FT_REGULAR);

   type file_access_t **is** (FA_READ, FA_WRITE, FA_EXECUTE);

   type access_permission_t **is** **array**(file_access_t)
              of boolean;
   type user_class_t **is** (UC_OWNER, UC_GROUP, UC_OTHERS);

   type access_list_t **is** **array**(user_class_t)
              of access_permission_t;

   type file_mode_t **is** **record**
       file_type : file_type_t;
       access_permissions : access_list_t;
   end record;

DIAGNOSTICS

   The constant NO_FILE is returned if: a needed directory is not searchable; the file does not exist and the directory in which it is to be created is not writable; the file does exist and is unwritable; the file is a directory;

EXEC(3)   PULSE Programmer's Manual   EXEC(3)

NAME

exec - execute a program

PACKAGE

fs_int

SYNOPSIS

procedure exec(s : string; his_fs : medium;
                lifeline : **out** medium;
                pri : priority; succ : **out** boolean);

DESCRIPTION

Exec causes the program contained in the named file, s , to be loaded locally and its execution commenced; his_fs is the file system request medium for the new program (previously allocated by a clone request); lifeline is a capability to a medium (owned by the new program) which is return to the caller and through which parameters to the new program may be sent. The priority of the new program is given by the value of pri.

COMPONENT TYPES

In package - fs_int_types

type priority_t **is** (FOREGROUND, BACKGROUND);

DIAGNOSTICS

If the file cannot be found, if it is not executable, or if it does not start with a valid magic number the value of the out parameter succ is FALSE.

LINK(3)   PULSE Programmer's Manual   LINK(3)

NAME

    link – link to a file

PACKAGE

    fs_int

SYNOPSIS

    function link(s1 : string; s2 : string) **return** boolean

DESCRIPTION

    A link to s1 is created; the link has the name s2. Either name may be an arbitrary path name.

DIAGNOSTICS

    TRUE is returned when a link is made; FALSE is returned when s1 cannot be found; when s2 already exists; when the directory of s2 cannot be written; when an attempt is made to link to a directory by a user other than the super-user; when an attempt is made to link to a file on another file volume; when a file has too many links.

LOCATE(3)   PULSE Programmer's Manual   LOCATE(3)

NAME

    locate – locate a medium associated with an open file

PACKAGE

    fs_int

SYNOPSIS

>**function** locate(file : file_t) **return** medium

DESCRIPTION

>Locate returns a medium which has been associated with a file by assert. File is an open file descriptor which has been returned by open.
>
>The caller must have opened the file for reading.

DIAGNOSTICS

>A NULL medium pointer is returned if there has been no prior assert on the file or the file is opened for writing only.

MAKE_DUP(3)　　　　　PULSE Programmer's Manual　　　　　MAKE_DUP(3)

NAME

>make_dup - make a local duplicate file

PACKAGE

>fs_int

SYNOPSIS

>**function** make_dup(sl : string) **return** boolean

DESCRIPTION

>Make_dup makes a local duplicate copy of the file sl. The file map setting must have local duplicate and remote master access enabled (see set_map).

DIAGNOSTICS

TRUE is returned if the duplicate has been successfully made. FALSE indicates that the file map setting was incorrect, the file does not exist, the duplicate file already exists or there is no space on the duplicate volume.

MKNOD(3) PULSE Programmer's Manual MKNOD(3)

NAME

mknod - make a directory or a special file

PACKAGE

fs_int

SYNOPSIS

function mknod(s : string; mode : file_mode_t) **return** boolean

DESCRIPTION

Mknod creates a new file whose name is s. The mode of the new file (including directory and special file bits) is initialized from mode.

Mknod may be invoked only by the super-user.

COMPONENT TYPES

In package - fs_int_types

```
type file_type_t is ( FT_DIR, FT_CHARACTER_SPECIAL,
    FT_BLOCK_SPECIAL, FT_REGULAR );

type file_access_t is ( FA_READ,
    FA_WRITE, FA_EXECUTE );

type access_permission_t is array(file_access_t)
        of boolean;
type user_class_t is (UC_OWNER, UC_GROUP, UC_OTHERS);

type access_list_t is array(user_class_t)
        of access_permission_t;

type file_mode_t is record
    file_type : file_type_t;
    access_permissions : access_list_t;
end record;
```

DIAGNOSTICS

TRUE is returned if the file has been made; FALSE if the file already exists or if the user is not the super-user.

BUGS

Special files are not supported by the file server.

NEWFS(3)   PULSE Programmer's Manual   NEWFS(3)

NAME

newfs - changes the file system request medium

PACKAGE

fs_int

SYNOPSIS

> **function** newfs(newmed : medium) **return** medium

DESCRIPTION

> Newfs changes the current file system request medium used by the fs_int package to be newmed (see clone). The old file system request medium is returned.

NOWAIT(3)　　　　　　PULSE Programmer's Manual　　　　　NOWAIT(3)

NAME

> nowait - do not wait for program to terminate

PACKAGE

> fs_int

SYNOPSIS

> **procedure** nowait(pid : integer);

DESCRIPTION

> Nowait informs the file server that the caller is not prepared to wait for the program pid to terminate (see also clone).

OPEN(3)   PULSE Programmer's Manual   OPEN(3)

NAME

open - open for reading or writing

PACKAGE

fs_int

SYNOPSIS

function open(s : string; m : open_mode_t) **return** file_t

DESCRIPTION

Open opens the file s for reading, writing or for both reading and writing.

The file is positioned at the beginning (byte 0). The returned open file descriptor must be used for subsequent calls for other input-output functions on the file.

COMPONENT TYPES

In package - fs_int_types.
type open_mode_t **is** (F_READ,
    F_WRITE, F_READ_AND_WRITE);

DIAGNOSTICS

The constant NO_FILE is returned if the file does not exist, if one of the necessary directories does not exist or is unreadable, if the file is not readable (resp. writable).

READ(3)　　　　　　PULSE Programmer's Manual　　　　　　READ(3)

NAME

    read - read from file

PACKAGE

    fs_int

SYNOPSIS

    function read(file : file_t; b : integer;
                 size : integer) **return** integer

DESCRIPTION

    File is an open file descriptor returned from a successful open or creat call. b is the location of size contiguous bytes into which the input will be placed. It is not guaranteed that all nbytes bytes will be read; for example if the file refers to a terminal at most one line will be returned. In any event the number of characters read is returned.

    If the returned value is 0, then end-of-file has been reached.

DIAGNOSTICS

    As mentioned, 0 is returned when the end of the file has been reached. If the read was otherwise unsuccessful the return value is -1.

RM_DUP(3)   PULSE Programmer's Manual   RM_DUP(3)

NAME

rm_dup - remove a local duplicate file

PACKAGE

fs_int

SYNOPSIS

function rm_dup(s1 : string) **return** boolean

DESCRIPTION

Rm_dup removes a local duplicate of the file s1. The file map setting must have local duplicate enabled (see set_map).

DIAGNOSTICS

TRUE is returned if the duplicate has bee successfully removed. FALSE indicates that the file map setting was incorrect or the duplicate file does not exist.

SEEK(3)   PULSE Programmer's Manual   SEEK(3)

NAME

seek - move read/write pointer

PACKAGE

fs_int

SYNOPSIS

function seek(file : file_t; offset : long_int;
                whence : seek_mode_t) **return** long_int

DESCRIPTION

   File refers to a file open for reading or writing. The returned value is the resulting pointer location.

COMPONENT TYPES

   In package - pstandard

   subtype long_int **is**integer;-- until in package standard

   In package - fs_int_types

   subtype offset_t **is** long_int;   -- file offset type

   type seek_mode_t **is** (S_START, S_CURRENT,
      S_END, S_BSTART, S_BCURRENT, S_BEND);

SET_MAP(3)   PULSE Programmer's Manual   SET_MAP(3)

NAME

   set_map - specify which file copies are to be accessed.

PACKAGE

   fs_int

SYNOPSIS

   procedure set_map(file_map : file_map_t)

DESCRIPTION

   When any file name is interpreted by the file server it attempts to access the various possible copies of the file in turn. Set_map informs the file server which particular locations and classes to consider.

   Note that any attempt to access a duplicate file copy for writing will always fail.

COMPONENT TYPES

In package – fs_int_types:

type file_location_t **is** (FL_LOCAL,FL_REMOTE);
type file_class_t **is** (FC_MASTER,FC_DUPLICATE);
type file_map_t **is array**(file_location_t,file_class_t)
    of boolean;

BUGS

Remote duplicate access is not yet supported by the file server. The order of access attempts is not user changeable (it is local master, local duplicate and remote master).

SET_RESULT(3)   PULSE Programmer's Manual   SET_RESULT(3)

NAME

set_result – set the return value of the program.

PACKAGE

fs_int

SYNOPSIS

procedure set_result(res : integer);

DESCRIPTION

Set result is the normal means of returning a result from a program to the parent (see also wait). A program terminates when its main procedure is exited but set result may be called at any time, all but the latest call being ignored.

STAT(3) PULSE Programmer's Manual STAT(3)

NAME

stat - get file status

PACKAGE

fs_int

SYNOPSIS

procedure stat(name : string; stbuf : **in out** stat_buf_t;
                  ok : **out** boolean)

DESCRIPTION

Stat obtains detailed information about a named file. Name is the file name. Stbuf is the buffer into which information is placed concerning the file. It is unnecessary to have any permissions at all with respect to the file, but all directories leading to the file must be searchable.

COMPONENT TYPES

In package - fs_int_types

```
type stat_buf_t is
   record
      device: device_t;
      global_ino : global_inumber_t;
      mode: file_mode_t;
      links : short_int;
      owner: owner_t;
      size: offset_t;
      rdev: device_t;
      access_time: time_t;
      mod_time: time_t;
      create_time: time_t;
      last_sync: time_t;
      remote: boolean;
      duplicate: boolean;
   end record;
```

```
type p_stat_buf_t is access stat_buf_t;
STAT_BUF_SIZE : constant integer :=
        (stat_buf_t'size/BYTE_SIZE);
subtype time_t is long_int;
subtype offset_t is long_int; --* file offset type
type file_type_t is ( FT_DIR, FT_CHARACTER_SPECIAL,
    FT_BLOCK_SPECIAL, FT_REGULAR );


type file_access_t is ( FA_READ,
    FA_WRITE, FA_EXECUTE );
type access_permission_t is
    array(file_access_t)of boolean;

type user_class_t is (UC_OWNER, UC_GROUP, UC_OTHERS);

type access_list_t is
    array(user_class_t) of access_permission_t;

type file_mode_t is record
    file_type : file_type_t;
    access_permissions : access_list_t;
end record;


In package - pulse_types

subtype volume_t is integer;         --* virtual volume
subtype inumber_t is short_natural; subtype isequence_t
is natural;

type global_inumber_t is record
    volume   : volume_t;
    inumber : inumber_t;
    isequence: isequence_t; end record;
```

DIAGNOSTICS

TRUE is returned in ok if a status is available; FALSE if the file cannot be found.

UNLINK(3)   PULSE Programmer's Manual   UNLINK(3)

NAME

    unlink - remove directory entry

PACKAGE

    fs_int

SYNOPSIS

    function unlink(s1 : string) **return** boolean

DESCRIPTION

    Unlink removes the entry for the named file s1 from its directory. If this entry was the last link to the file, the contents of the file are freed and the file is destroyed. If, however, the file was open in any process, the actual destruction is delayed until it is closed, even though the directory entry has disappeared.

DIAGNOSTICS

    TRUE is normally returned; FALSE indicates that the file does not exist, or that its directory cannot be written. Write permission is not required on the file itself. It is also illegal to unlink a directory (except for the super-user).

WAIT(3)   PULSE Programmer's Manual   WAIT(3)

NAME

    wait - wait for program to terminate

PACKAGE

    fs_int

SYNOPSIS

    function wait(pid : integer) **return** exit_status_t;

DESCRIPTION

    Wait causes its caller to delay until the program which is identifed by pid terminates. The program's exit status is returned, this comprises the user (see set result) and kernel result values.

COMPONENT TYPES

    In package - fs_int_types.

    type exit_status_t **is**
       record
          u_val : integer;
          k_val : integer;
       end record;

BUGS

    The exit status is not yet reported.

WRITE(3)　　　　　PULSE Programmer's Manual　　　　　WRITE(3)

NAME

write - write on a file

PACKAGE

fs_int

SYNOPSIS

function write(file : file_t; b : integer;
        size : integer) **return** integer

DESCRIPTION

File is an open file descriptor returned from a successful open, or creat call.

B is the address of size contiguous bytes which are written on the output file. The number of characters actually written is returned. It should be regarded as an error if this is not the same as requested.

DIAGNOSTICS

Returns -1 on error: bad descriptor, buffer address, or count; physical I/O errors.

Appendix C: A REVIEW OF ADA TASKING

The Ada language is the result of several years of analysis of the requirements for programming embedded computer systems. It has progressed from the original Green language[49] to the current ANSI standard Ada[23]. The language has many new and interesting features not least of which are its facilities for multi-tasking. It was because of this that Ada was chosen as the principal implementation language for the PULSE project. Our actual experience in using tasking has shown up unforeseen problems with the language. Although much has been written on tasking[12,98,95,108,105], attention has centred mainly on the efficiency of possible implementations[104,38,37,55,40,29]. In this appendix, we intend to examine the model itself and present some of the problems we and others have experienced.

In section C.1 we discuss the overall tasking model. In section C.2 a methodology, developed by Bloom, for evaluating synchronisation primitives is described and then applied to the Ada rendezvous. The conclusions that may be drawn from our work are then presented in section C.3.

C.1 The Tasking Model

The unit of parallelism is called a task. They are explicitly declared objects and can be created by the use of task access types and the "new" operation, or by declaration on task or scope entry. An example of the latter case is the creation and activation of tasks on entry to a procedure.

Following Pyle[86], we use the concept of passive and active tasks. Passive tasks provide a set of services and active tasks call for these services as required. A task may be both active and passive at different times in its life.

C.1.1 Communication and Synchronisation

Communication and synchronisation between tasks are achieved using a rendezvous mechanism. The actions are as follows:

- Tasks proceed independently until they wish to synchronise and communicate.

- Either task must wait at the appropriate synchronisation point for the other to arrive.

- One task (the active task) issues an entry call naming the other (the passive task).

- The passive task states that it is prepared to "accept" communication from any task. The calling task is chosen. The tasks are now synchronised; the called task takes the parameters passed by the calling task and continues its execution. It then passes back any results to the calling task, at which point both tasks carry on independently.

Ada is similar to DP[14] in that it presents an asymmetric naming scheme. The active task has to name the task with which it wishes to rendezvous, whereas the passive task merely states that it is prepared to take part in general communication. This asymmetry was justified in the Rationale for the Green Language[48] because it allowed a general library routine to provide a service for an arbitrary user task. In a scheme where tasks must name each other, such as CSP[41], the server task must enumerate all possible users. An indirect naming scheme, where each task names a passive object such as a Link[7] or a Port[4] was rejected because it introduced an additional language construct and required a dual connection mechanism[48]. To achieve indirect naming a buffer task may be introduced between the two communicating tasks. In such a program both tasks might name the buffer but they would be communicating with each other.

The entry and accept mechanisms enable a task to wait for an event to happen; the event is the corresponding task's accept or entry call. The select statement allows a passive task to wait simultaneously for one of several entries to occur. If none of the entries is available the task has the option of executing an "else" clause, delaying for a period of time, or terminating itself. If more than one entry is available to the select, one of them is selected arbitrarily (that is, the language does not define which one). For active tasks the select statement only allows entry calls to be made with a specified timeout or with the "else" option; such calls are termed delayed and conditional entry calls. Here again the rendezvous mechanism is asymmetric in that it allows the passive task to wait simultaneously for several entry calls while the active task can only issue one entry call at a time.

Figure C.1, from page 9-14 of the Language Reference Manual (LRM)[23], illustrates the basic rendezvous mechanism. It shows a task which controls access to a shared resource by means of a Boolean variable. The controlling task loops accepting a request to seize or release the resource. Notice that once the resource has been seized then the branch of the select which accepted that request is closed. The accept statement is said to be guarded. In Ada the guard can only be a Boolean expression.

```
task resource is
    entry seize;
    entry release;
end resource;

task body resource is
    busy : boolean := FALSE;
begin
    loop
        select
            when not busy =>
                accept seize do
                    busy := TRUE;
                end;
        or
            accept release do
                busy := FALSE;
            end;
        or
            terminate;
        end select;
    end loop;
end resource;
```

Figure C.1: A Simple Resource Controller

The calling task requests access to the resource; once this has been obtained it uses the resource and then returns it. In Figure C.2 if the calling task fails to access the resource in ten seconds it withdraws the request. The construct is called a "timed entry call".

```
task resource_requester;

task body resource_requester is
begin
    select
        resource.seize;
        -- use resource
        resource.release;
    or
        delay 10.0;
    end select;
end resource_requester;
```

Figure C.2: A Resource Requester Task

Notice that if the rendezvous is entered then the calling task is committed; it must wait until the rendezvous has been completed. In Ada it is not possible for the timeout value to be associated with the return of control. Once held within the rendezvous the calling task has no way of withdrawing. In the Green language tasks were not even allowed to withdraw the entry call; once issued they were committed unless they were aborted.

C.1.2 Task Types and Task Access Variables

A number of identical tasks can be created by declaring a task type and then using it to declare several task objects. For the resource manager example a task type would be declared as follows:

```
task type resource is
    entry seize;
    entry release;
end resource;
```

An object of this type may be declared in the same fashion as any other Ada object defined by a type. However a task type is "limited private": objects of it have access neither to assignment nor to the predefined comparison for equality.

An access variable for a task type can also be defined, thereby allowing tasks to be created dynamically using an "allocator".

```
type resource_name is access resource;

a_resource : resource_name;

begin
    a_resource := new resource;
end;
```

C.1.3 Entry Family

An entry declaration that includes a "discrete range" declares a family of distinct entries. (See Figure C.7 for an example of an entry family: the "discrete range" in this case is an enumerated type.) All the entries in the family have the same parameters and are identified by an index. Only individual entries may be referenced in a rendezvous; if a task wishes to wait simultaneously for an entry call from several members of the family, the select statement must enumerate them all.

C.1.4 Task Abortion

A task can be aborted using the abort statement. There are no "last wishes" associated with this facility; that is, a task cannot trap the abort and carry out a final operation before being terminated. However, there are certain conditions when the abortion of a task does not take place immediately. For example, if a task is aborted after it has issued an entry call and the rendezvous is in progress, the abortion does not take place until the rendezvous has terminated.

A task which has been aborted is said to be abnormal. With such a task any attempted rendezvous will result in the exception "tasking_error" being raised in the calling task. If, however, the called task is waiting for communication and the calling task goes abnormal there is no way that the called task can be informed. In this case the called task must use the delay option of the select statement to timeout the call if it has not been received within a certain period.

C.1.5 Task Attributes

A task has several attributes: 'callable', 'terminated' and 'count'. The first two indicate whether the task is completed, terminated or abnormal. The third, when applied to a specific entry of a task, indicates the number of calls queued on that entry.

C.2 Evaluation of the Rendezvous

In recent years there have been many proposed synchronisation mechanisms from Dijkstra's semaphores to Hoare's monitors. Although each claims to have advantages over its predecessors there have been no accepted criteria for evaluating their effectiveness. For the purpose of this appendix we shall use the criteria developed by Bloom.

C.2.1 Requirements for a Synchronisation Mechanism

Bloom[10] has divided the requirements for a synchronisation mechanism into three areas: modularity, expressive power and ease of use. It is these requirements that we use to evaluate the Ada rendezvous.

C.2.1.1 Modularity

There are two modularity requirements that should be satisfied when concurrent programs are synchronising and communicating through a shared resource. The first is that the definition of the resource should be separated from its use. This implies that the implementation of the shared resource should define the operations on the resource, the synchronisation scheme and the resource's internal structure. This encapsulation allows the user of the resource to assume its proper synchronisation without needing synchronisation code at each point of access. (In embedded computer applications this may not be the case as the user of the resource may need to be aware that a delay in its access may occur and wish to take alternative actions.)

The other requirement of modularity governs the structure of the shared resource definition. The operations on the resource are independent of whether the resource is accessed concurrently; they should be separated from the mechanisms which provide the synchronisation.

C.2.1.2 Expressive Power and Ease of Use

There are two types of synchronisation when communication occurs using shared variables[3]. The first is "mutual exclusion" which ensures that a sequence of statements is treated as an indivisible operation. The second is "condition synchronisation" where a process attempting an operation might be delayed until the state of the data controlled by that operation changes as a result of another process's execution. This is sometimes referred to as "resource scheduling". The expressive power of the synchronisation mechanism is defined to be the ability to express the constraints on condition synchronisation. The ease of use is defined to be the ease with which the constraints may be combined to implement complex resource allocation problems.

There are several categories of information concerning the resource which constrain the condition synchronisation; they are as follows.

1) The type of request.

   The resource is a data abstraction that can only be accessed through operations. Imposing restrictions on the ordering of those operations according to the type of operation (for example giving readers to a resource priority over writers) will affect how the resource is scheduled.

2) The relative ordering of the request.

   When users are queuing for operations on the resource, some information concerning how long requests have been waiting is usually required by the synchroniser in order to avoid starvation of a particular user.

3) Request parameters.

   Often the parameters with a request may affect the order in which those requests are satisfied. For example where resources are allocated from a pool several at a time, a request for a small number may be serviced before a request for a larger number.

4) The "synchronised state" of the resource.

   Only certain operations may be available on a resource if it has already been allocated to a process.

5) The local state of the resource.

   Information concerning the local state of the resource has no direct relevance to its concurrent access but is required by the synchroniser. For example it may indicate whether a pool of resources is exhausted or that a buffer is full.

C.2.2 Bloom's Methodology Applied to Ada

C.2.2.1 Modularity Requirements

Tasking by itself does not satisfy Bloom's two modularity requirements. Although the resource definition can be separated from its use, the synchronisation scheme cannot be hidden. It is not possible to encapsulate the resource, the operations on the resource and its synchronisation. It is also not possible to separate the resource's implementation from the mechanism used for synchronisation*. However, when taken together with the Ada package both requirements may be completely satisfied.

The package provides the necessary encapsulation allowing only the operations on the resource to be visible in the specification. The implementation and the synchronisation strategy may be hidden from the user in the package body. In the package body, the implementation of the resource can be separated from the task providing the synchronisation.

For example, consider a simple resource which may be allocated and released. In Ada this may be represented by the package shown in Figure C.3.

---

*In the Green Language a task could meet all the modularity requirements.

```ada
package resource_manager is

    type resource is private;
    function allocate return resource;
    procedure free(this_resource : resource);

private
    type resource is  .....
end resource_manager;

package body resource_manager is

    task manager is
        entry allocate_resource;
        entry free_resource;
    end manager;

    task body manager is
    begin
        -- code to control access
        -- to resource
    end manager;

    function allocate return resource is
    begin
        -- code of the operation
        -- allocate
    end allocate;

    procedure free(this_resource : resource) is
    begin
        -- code of operation;
        -- free
    end free;

end resource_manager;
```

Figure C.3: A Resource Manager Package

The resource and the operations are defined by the package specification. The implementation of the operations allocate and free is separated from the manager task which controls the synchronisation.

C.2.2.2 Expressive Power

Mutual exclusion in Ada is given by the rendezvous mechanism; one task, the passive task, accepts an entry call on behalf of an active task to grant access to a resource. As only the passive task can access the resource directly, mutual exclusion is ensured.

To evaluate the "expressive power" of the Ada tasking primitives each constraint on condition synchronisation is taken and the corresponding Ada construct is given.

The Type of the Request

Imposing restrictions on the ordering of operations can be achieved in Ada by having a separate entry in the manager task for each operation. These entries may be controlled by a select statement; where necessary each entry may have an associated guard. For example consider the case where the readers to a resource have priority over the writers, given in Figure C.4

```
task manager is
    entry read;
    entry write;
end manager;

task body manager is
begin
    loop
        select
            accept read;
        or
            when read'count = 0 =>
                accept write;
        end select;
    end loop;
end manager;
```

Figure C.4: Giving Priority to the Read Operation

The select statement selects between the two operations read and write. Readers are given priority by the guard on the write operation. The write entry will only be opened if there are no readers queued on the read operation.

Unfortunately, this example may not achieve the desired results as the execution of the select statement is not an indivisible action. Consider the case when there is a single task queued on the read entry. When the guard to the write operation is evaluated, "read´count" is equal to 1 so any write entry calls are inhibited. If at this point the task queued on the read entry times out or is aborted, the select statement will block waiting for another read entry call. This results in the unnecessary blocking of tasks queued on the write entry call; at best they will just be delayed, at worst the system will deadlock.

The Relative Ordering of Events

For each operation the requests are queued on a first-come-first-served basis at the entry associated with the request. This is guaranteed by the language.

Given more than one request, each of which is represented by a single entry call, it is not possible in Ada to choose the oldest. Although the select statement provides a mechanism for accepting one of several requests, there is no way of expressing the order in which all the outstanding requests are to be serviced. When a task executes a select statement and there are several alternatives available, the language does not define the order in which they are accepted. Indirectly this may be done by combining the requests into a single request and using the same entry.

The Synchronised State of the Resource

This constraint may be expressed by a guard to the accept statement. For example a manager which will only accept a call to free a resource, when the resource is allocated, is expressed in Figure C.5

```
task body manager is
begin
   ..
   ..
   if resource = allocated then
       accept free;
   end if;
   ..
   ..
end manager;
```

Figure C.5: Expressing the Synchronised State as a Constraint on the Rendezvous

The "if statement" only allows a call for freeing the resource to be accepted if the resource has already been allocated.

A more difficult example occurs when the task freeing the resource must be the task to which it was allocated. In Ada it is not possible to express the identity of the calling task in the guard to the call, indeed the identity may be unknown. Welsh and Lister[108] have discussed ways of circumventing this particular problem and the difficulties that are introduced. The basic solution requires returning a key, which is private to the manager, when the resource is allocated. This key must be presented when the resource is freed. All operations from tasks which attempt to free the resource with an invalid key are rejected.

The Local State of the Resource

This again can be expressed as a guard to the accept statement. For example, consider the case when a manager to a buffer cannot accept any more requests to write to the buffer because the buffer is already full. The example is shown in Figure C.6.

```
task body manager is
begin
    ..
    ..
    if buffer /= full then
        accept write;
    end if;
    ..
    ..
end manager;
```

Figure C.6: Expressing the Local State as a Constraint on the Rendezvous

A solution for condition synchronisation constrained by history information is similar.

The Request Parameters

This constraint has been left until last because it is the one which cannot be expressed in Ada. The standard solution for providing condition synchronisation has been to use a guard to an accept statement to prevent the entry being accepted if the constraint does not hold. In a previous subsection it was established that the identity of the calling task cannot be expressed in the guard which controls the entry. Similarly, in Ada the guard cannot contain the parameters to the potential request. The only way that a task can distinguish between calls to the same entry is to associate a family with that entry.

Consider the case where each request has an associated priority as a parameter. When there is a small number of priority levels the solution is given in Figure C.7. (This solution is adapted from that given in the Rationale for the Green Language[48] page 11-21.)

```
type level is (URGENT, MEDIUM, LOW);

task manager is
    entry request(level'first .. level'last);
end manager;

task body manager is
begin
    ..
    select
        accept request(URGENT);
    or
        when (request(URGENT)'count = 0) =>
            accept request(MEDIUM);
    or
        when (request(URGENT)'count = 0) and
            (request(MEDIUM)'count = 0) =>
            accept request(LOW);
    end select;
    ..
end manager;
```

Figure C.7: Using a Family of Entries to Express
Request Parameter Constraints on the Rendezvous

The manager declares a family of entries and then enumerates each member in the select statement. The guard placed on the MEDIUM member's entry ensures that a call is not accepted if there are any outstanding calls on the URGENT entry. The guard placed on the LOW member's entry ensures that a call is not accepted while there are any outstanding calls for either of the other two entries.

However, as shown in the description of Figure C.4, the use of the "count" attribute does not guarantee that the lower priority calls are not blocked when higher priority calls have timed out or have been aborted. Furthermore, for a larger number of priority levels it is not desirable to enumerate all the members in the family. Figure C.8 shows an alternative approach, suggested by the Rationale (page 11-22). For convenience this example has line numbers.

```ada
 1 package resource_manager is
 2    subtype level is integer range 1..50;
 3    procedure request(priority : level);
 4 end resource_manager;
 5
 6 package body resource_manager is
 7
 8    task manager is
 9       entry sign_in(priority : level);
10       entry perform(level'first .. level'last);
11    end manager;
12
13    procedure request(priority : level) is
14    begin
15       manager.sign_in(priority);
16       manager.perform(priority);
17    end request;
18
19    task body manager is
20
21       pending : array(level'first .. level'last) of
22               integer := (level'first .. level'last => 0);
23       total : integer := 0;
24    begin
25       loop
26          if total = 0 then
27             -- no request to be served:
28             -- wait if necessary.
29             accept sign_in(priority : level) do
30                pending(priority):=pending(priority)+1;
31                total := 1;
32             end sign_in;
33          end if;
34          loop -- accept any pending signin don't wait
35             select
36                accept sign_in(priority : level) do
37                   pending(priority):=pending(priority)+1;
38                   total := total +1;
39                end sign_in;
40             else
41                exit;
42             end select;
43          end loop;
44
```

Review of Ada Tasking

```
45            for i in reverse level'first..level'last loop
46               if pending(i) > 0 then
47                  accept perform(i);
48                  pending(i) := pending(i) -1;
49                  total := total -1;
50                  exit;  --loop to accept new request
51               end if;
52            end loop;
53         end loop;
54      end manager;
55 end resource_manager;
```

Figure C.8: Using a Two Stage Interaction to Express Request Parameter Constraints on the Rendezvous

In order to service a request a two stage interaction with the manager is required: a "sign in" request and a perform request. This may be hidden from the user of the resource by encapsulating the manager in a package and providing a single procedure to handle the request* (lines 1-4).

When there are no outstanding calls the manager waits for a "sign in" request (lines 26-33). When one arrives its priority is noted (line 30) in the array of pending requests (lines 21-22). A loop is entered to record all the "sign in" requests that may be outstanding (lines 34-43). Notice that this loop terminates as soon as there are no more by using a conditional select statement (lines 35-42) with an exit in the else clause (line 41).

The "for" loop (lines 45-52) is then used to scan through the pending table and the operation with the highest priority is accepted (line 47). The main loop (lines 25 - 53) is then repeated in case a higher priority request has attempted to sign in.

---

*This is a good example of the modularity offered by combining tasking and packages. The user of the resource assumes that it is synchronised. No code is present at the call.

This solution is complicated, as it requires the double interaction, and it is expensive as an entry is required for every possible priority. Unfortunately, it is not complete; no account is taken of the possibility of the task being aborted after signing in but before the operation has been performed. The solution presented will deadlock at the accept statement on line 47 when the only outstanding call at that priority has been aborted.

As presented this example does not provide a general solution even if it were resilient in the face of the abortion of the requesting task. The range of the parameter is still restricted. If the parameter were an arbitrary integer its range could be enormous and it would not be feasible for a task to have that many entries.

Summary of Expressive Power

The rendezvous mechanism has been shown to be capable of expressing 5 out of the 6 constraints identified by Bloom. The mechanism for expressing the parameter constraint has no direct expression in Ada.

Two less important problems have also been discovered: the ordering of events for several different operations on a first-come-first-served basis is only possible if all the operations are mapped onto the same entry; and problems have been encountered when the identity of the calling task is needed to validate its request.

C.2.2.3 Ease of Use

The term "ease of use" really means "ease of combination of synchronisation conditions". The degree of interaction (or even conflict) of the expression of the different synchronisation conditions has a direct bearing on the difficulty of solving a particular problem. We have shown that Ada lacks expressive power in relation to request parameters: this being so, it is difficult to evaluate "ease of use" as suggested by Bloom. Instead we have selected a problem which requires the combination of several constraints, and present here example implementations of a suitable management scheme. One constraint is concerned with the request parameters: it has been suggested that although Ada lacks explicit means of expression in this respect, problems can be solved by combining other language primitives. We have deliberately placed importance on this so that some measure can be made of Ada's strength in solving such problems.

The Example

The example concerns a request for several resources to be allocated from and returned to a pool. It requires that condition synchronisation is subject to the following constraints:

1) the type of request (allocate or free),

2) the parameter to the allocate request which contains the number of resources to be allocated,

3) and the resource's synchronisation state — that is how many resources are available for allocation.

The actual problem is that of allocating space on a disk. The resource manager is encapsulated in a package whose specification is given by Figure C.9.

package disk_allocator **is**

    function dalloc(size : natural) **return** disk_address;
    procedure dfree(addr :disk_address);

end disk_allocator;

Figure C.9: The Disk Allocator Package Specification

Only the operations allocate and free are visible; the user of the package assumes that adequate synchronisation is provided by the package body. The type "disk_address" is an integer type defined elsewhere: objects of this type must be used for operations on the disk. The allocation algorithm will keep track of the sizes of allocated data. This means that "dfree" need only use the disk address returned by a previous call to "dalloc": there is no mechanism for freeing other amounts of space. The detail of the actual allocation algorithm is not relevant to the problem and is not described.

Assumptions and Conditions

The algorithms presented assume that tasks holding resources are normally well-behaved in that they do not attempt to return resources that are either not allocated, or allocated to another task. However, all resources allocated from the pool are assumed to be returned unless a holding task fails. In this case the resources are assumed to be lost.

Furthermore, the following conditions are imposed for a solution to be considered valid.

1) A requester must never be made to wait if sufficient resources are available and the manager is not otherwise occupied. Also neither the requester nor the manager must "busy wait" as this would not be in the spirit of Ada.

2) The solution must be resilient in the face of the failure or abortion of a requesting task. Only if the managing task fails should the system deadlock. Furthermore, no situation must arise that prevents a requesting task from being aborted by another.

3) If resources are lost at any time, the manager must continue with a depleted pool.

The Approach

It has already been shown that condition synchronisation constrained by parameters in a request cannot be directly expressed in Ada. The request must therefore be accepted and if possible serviced immediately; if not the requester must be requeued on a different entry. Four solutions are now presented and the merits and failings of each are examined.

First Ada Solution

The essence of this solution, presented in Figure C.10, is that the requesters take the initiative over competing for resources.

On receipt of a "dalloc" request (lines 10-18), the rendezvous "alloc" is made (lines 44-46). If space is available, then the address of the new block is returned. If the first "alloc" rendezvous returns a "NO_SPACE" address, the requester must call the "retry" entry. When resources become available, all the retry rendezvous are completed, and the callers compete for the newly freed storage.

The managing task keeps no explicit state information. In general, tasks will be requeued on entry "retry" in the order that requests are made, and as such are serviced on a "first-come-first-served" policy.

```ada
 1  package body disk_allocator is
 2
 3     NO_SPACE : constant integer := -1;
 4     task manager is
 5        entry alloc(size : natural; addr : out integer);
 6        entry free(addr : disk_address);
 7        entry retry(size : natural; addr : out integer);
 8     end manager;
 9
10     function dalloc(size:natural) return disk_address is
11        local_addr : integer;
12     begin
13        manager.alloc(size, local_addr);
14        while local_addr = NO_SPACE loop
15           manager.retry(size, local_addr);
16        end loop;
17        return disk_address(local_addr);
18     end dalloc;
19
20     procedure dfree(addr : disk_address) is
21     begin
22        manager.free(addr);
23     end;
24
25     function local_alloc(size:natural) return integer is
26     begin
27        -- Calls are mutually exclusive
28        -- Actually allocates the space.
29        -- If none return NO_SPACE
30     end local_alloc;
31
32
33
34     procedure local_free(addr : disk_address) is
35     begin
36        -- return space to the pool
37     end local_free;
```

```
38
39      task body manager is
40      begin
41         loop
42            select
43
44               accept alloc(size : natural;
45                            addr : out integer) do
46                  addr := local_alloc(size);
47               end alloc;
48            or
49
50               accept free(addr : disk_address) do
51                  local_free(addr);
52               end free;
53               for i in 1 .. retry'count loop
54                  select
55                     accept retry(size : natural;
56                                  addr : out integer) do
57                        addr := local_alloc(size);
58                     end retry;
59                  else
60                     exit;
61                  end select;
62               end loop;
63            end select;
64         end loop;
65      end manager;
66
67 end disk_allocator;
```

Figure C.10: Disk Allocator - First Solution

The solution is in the style of that given (p11-23) in the original rationale for Ada[48]. It satisfies conditions 2 and 3 above, in that failure of a requesting task is handled gracefully. If a task dies after making an unsatisfied request, but before issuing the retry entry (line 15), the managing task is not affected, since retry'count is not updated. Once the rendezvous is made the managing task behaves as follows. When failure occurs before the loop (lines 53 -64) is entered, then the count of tasks on the retry entry (line 55) will be decremented. However, once that loop is entered, the loop's termination value has been evaluated (line 53), and will not be changed even though the count of the tasks on the retry entry may do so. The use of a conditional select (lines 54 - 61) avoids the possibility of the manager waiting for a non-existent entry. Only if an entry is already waiting will the rendezvous be accepted, otherwise the loop will terminate (line 60).

This example suffers from the major deficiency that races may occur between tasks requesting and freeing resources. Since a task must be rescheduled between the "alloc" and "retry" rendezvous, it is possible that another task may free resources, and the current queue of retries be cleared, before the first task can be placed on the retry queue. Therefore a task may be waiting in the retry queue even though resources are available. This clearly violates our first condition of operation. No direct variant of this example avoids this problem because there is no means of closing entry "free" temporarily while a task is being queued on entry "retry".

Second Ada Solution

The main problem with the first solution was that the "count" attribute of the retry entry was used to determine the number of outstanding requests. The second Ada solution presented in Figure C.11 counts the number of outstanding requests explicitly.

```ada
 1  package body disk_allocator is
 2
 3     NO_SPACE : constant integer := -1;
 4     total : integer := 0;
 5     task manager is
 6        entry alloc(size : natural; addr : out integer);
 7        entry free(addr : disk_address);
 8        entry retry(size : natural; addr : out integer);
 9     end manager;
10
11     function dalloc(size:natural) return disk_address is
12        local_addr : integer;
13     begin
14        manager.alloc(size, local_addr);
15        while local_addr = NO_SPACE loop
16              manager.retry(size, local_addr);
17        end loop;
18        return disk_address(local_addr);
19     end dalloc;
20
21     procedure dfree(addr : disk_address) is
22     begin
23        manager.free(addr);
24     end;
25
26     function local_alloc(size:natural) return integer is
27     begin
28        -- Calls are mutually exclusive
29        -- Actually allocates the space.
30        -- If none return NO_SPACE
31     end local_alloc;
32
33     procedure local_free(addr : disk_address) is
34     begin
35        -- return space to the pool
36     end local_free;
37
```

```
38     task body manager is
39        local_addr : integer;
40     begin
41        loop
42           select
43              accept alloc(size : natural;
44                       addr : out integer) do
45                 local_addr := local_alloc(size);
46                 if local_addr = NO_SPACE then
47                    total := total+1;
48                 end if;
49                 addr := local_addr;
50              end alloc;
51           or
52              accept free(addr : disk_address) do
53                 local_free(addr);
54              end free;
55              for i in 1 .. total loop
56
57                 accept  retry(size : natural;
58                          addr : out integer) do
59                    local_addr := local_alloc(size);
60                    if local_addr /= NO_SPACE then
61                       total := total -1;
62                    end if;
63                    addr := local_addr;
64                 end retry;
65
66              end loop;
67           end select;
68        end loop;
69     end manager;
70 end disk_allocator;
```

Figure C.11: Disk Allocator – Second Solution

Although races are avoided by waiting for the retry entry call (lines 57-64) this solution suffers from the same problem as the example given in Figure C.8; if the requesting task is aborted, after attempting to allocate a resource but before being allocated, then the manager deadlocks on line 57.

Third Ada Solution

This example is both resilient and avoids races. The two previous solutions each had a managing task which performed a monitor-like function: it did not make entry calls but waited passively for requests. This solution, presented in Figure C.12, has a managing task which accepts requests, but calls an entry to grant the resources (lines 60-64). Each request causes the creation of an intermediate task (lines 17) which handles the responses from the manager (lines 37-40) and the giving of the resource to the calling task (lines 37-40).

```ada
 1  package body disk_allocator is
 2
 3     task type allocator_t is
 4          entry disk_avail(p : disk_address);
 5          entry results(p : out disk_address);
 6     end allocator_t;
 7     type allocator is access allocator_t;
 8     task manager is
 9        entry alloc(size : natural; tp : allocator);
10        entry free(pointer : disk_address);
11     end manager;
12
13     function dalloc(size:natural)return disk_address is
14        local_pointer : disk_address;
15        tp            : allocator;
16     begin
17        tp := new allocator_t;
18        manager.alloc(size,tp);
19        tp.results(local_pointer);
20        return local_pointer;
21     end dalloc;
22
23     procedure dfree(pointer : disk_address) is
24     begin
25        manager.free(pointer);
26     end dfree;
27
28
29
30     task body allocator_t is
31        localp : disk_address;
32     begin
33       accept disk_avail(p : disk_address) do
34          localp := p;
35       end disk_avail;
36
37       accept results(p : out disk_address) do
38          p := localp;
39       end results;
40     end allocator_t;
41
42
```

```
43      task body manager is
44         p : disk_address;
45      begin
46         loop
47            select
48               accept alloc(size : natural;
49                            tp : allocator) do
50                  -- if enough space is available, allocate
51                  -- it and make return entry immediately.
52                  -- tp.disk_avail(p);
53                  -- if not, record details of request
54               end alloc;
55
56            or
57               accept free(pointer : disk_address) do
58                  -- free storage
59               end free;
60               -- if we can satisfy outstanding
61               -- requests do so, waiting if necessary
62               -- atp.disk_avail(p);
63               -- handle tasking exceptions
64               -- if task disappears
65            end select;
66         end loop;
67      end manager;
68 end disk_allocator;
```

Figure C.12: Disk Allocator - Third Solution

This solution satisfies all three conditions, but is expensive in space and execution time: each request causes several context switches and the creation of a task. Unlike the previous examples, the manager maintains state information about pending requests, and sends the resources to the most suitable candidate.

Races are avoided since the granting of resources is performed actively by the manager. The solution is also resilient in the face of both calling and intermediate task failure. If the calling task fails while holding resources then, as before, those resources are lost to the pool. If it fails after creating the worker task or while awaiting the results of a request, the cost is that of the idle intermediate task. In the former case no resources are lost from the pool.

Although it would seem that this last example has resolved the problems encountered in the previous two, albeit at some expense, it is still not acceptable. The intermediate task will remain even if the calling task dies before it can issue a request to the manager. Moreover, there is a hidden cost imposed by the rules in Ada which govern the accessibility and visibility of a task created using an access variable. Because the task type is declared at the outermost level of the package, the compiler cannot know that the manager task is going to discard the task access variable after the satisfaction of a "dalloc" request. The language definition states that tasks of a type so declared remain potentially accessible, with the implication that the run-time support system must keep some associated storage intact. It follows that each call of dalloc, whether successful or not, will result in the creation of a task, some part of which will never disappear. As there is no requirement in the LRM for a garbage collector, the program will eventually run out of space. Indeed it may well be impractical for a real-time language to allow garbage collection because the execution time overheads are heavy and unpredictable[114].

Fourth Ada Solution

The following variation of the previous example. Figure C.13, restricts the parallelism by creating a fixed number of intermediate tasks at package elaboration time. Each call to dalloc would then be allocated one of these tasks, which later would be returned to the pool. This mechanism avoids the need for a garbage collector.

```ada
package body disk_allocator is
    MAX_WORKERS : constant natural := 10;
    type wk_range is  range 1 .. MAX_WORKERS;
    task type allocator_t is
        entry my_id(id : wk_range);
        entry disk_avail(p : disk_address);
        entry results(p : out disk_address);
    end allocator_t;
    type allocator is access allocator_t;
    type worker_tasks is array(wk_range) of allocator;
    workers : worker_tasks;

    task worker_manager is
        entry get_worker(tp : out allocator);
        entry worker_available(id : wk_range);
    end worker_manager;
    task disk_manager is
        entry alloc(size : natural; tp : allocator);
        entry free(pointer : disk_address);
    end disk_manager;

    function dalloc(size : natural) return disk_address is
        local_pointer : disk_address;
        tp       : allocator;
    begin
        worker_manager.get_worker(tp);
        disk_manager.alloc(size,tp);
        tp.results(local_pointer);
        return local_pointer;
    end dalloc;

    procedure dfree(pointer : disk_address) is
    begin
        disk_manager.free(pointer);
    end dfree;
```

```ada
task body allocator_t is
    localp : disk_address;
    myid : wk_range;
begin
    accept my_id(id : wk_range) do
        myid := id;
    end my_id;
    loop
        worker_manager.worker_available(myid);
        accept disk_avail(p : disk_address) do
            localp := p;
        end disk_avail;
        accept results(p : out disk_address) do
            p := localp;
        end results;
    end loop;
end allocator_t;

task body worker_manager is
begin
    loop
        accept get_worker(tp : out allocator) do
            accept worker_available(id : wk_range) do
                tp := workers(id);
            end worker_available;
        end get_worker;
    end loop;
end worker_manager;
```

```
       task body disk_manager is
           p : disk_address;
       begin
           loop
               select
                   accept alloc(size : natural;
                                tp : allocator) do
                       -- if enough space is available,
                       -- allocate it and make return
                       -- entry immediately
                       -- tp.disk_avail(p);
                       -- if not, record details of request
                   end alloc;
               or
                   accept free(pointer : disk_address) do
                       -- free storage
                   end free;
                   -- if we can satisfy outstanding
                   -- requests do so, waiting if necessary
                   -- atp.disk_avail(p);
                   -- handle tasking exceptions if task
                   -- disappears
               end select;
           end loop;
       end disk_manager;
   begin
       for i in wk_range loop
           workers(i) := new allocator_t;
           workers(i).my_id(i);
       end loop;
   end disk_allocator;
```

Figure C.13: Disk Allocator - Fourth Solution

However, this solution still has shortcomings; in order that condition 1 is met, the pool of intermediate tasks must be sufficient to handle the projected load; otherwise a request may be forced to wait even though space is available*. If a calling task fails after being allocated an intermediate task, that worker task is lost to the pool. A

---
*Dynamically building the pool would avoid this problem.

possible remedy is to make the worker return itself to the pool if no request comes within a long period but again this introduces a theoretical race condition.

Summary of Ease of Use

The resource allocation example presented in this section is not inherently difficult. An efficient and elegant solution may be found in languages where synchronisation and communication is based on Monitors[63]. In Ada, however, it appears there is no satisfactory algorithm which, on the one hand, is both resilient in the face of failures and avoids race conditions and, on the other, does not require garbage collection. The problems are a direct result of the interaction of the four following features of Ada.

1) A task must accept an entry call before it knows whether it can satisfy any request contained within it. That is, a guard of a select cannot contain the parameters of an entry.

2) Once a rendezvous has commenced it is not possible to requeue a calling task directly: that task must requeue itself.

3) A task can be aborted unconditionally by any other.

4) In general, an accepting task is unaware of the identity of a task making entries to it.

The problem requires a manager to accept a request before it knows whether it can satisfy it (Feature 1). If the request must then wait it must be queued at another accept. This is the responsibility of the requesting task (Feature 2). The consequence is that races may occur between the end of the first (unsuccessful) rendezvous and the requeuing of the request. Keeping status information about unsatisfied requests avoids the races. However, (Feature 3) means that a task can be aborted while a request is pending, but because of (Feature 4) the manager cannot know that an open retry accept may never be entered. The only answer is for the manager actively to send the results to a known intermediate task, which in turn makes them available to the requester. The ensuing solution is inelegant and inefficient.

C.3 Conclusions

Although Ada has been able to satisfy Bloom's Modularity requirements it has fallen short on expressive power and consequently on ease of use. The Ada rendezvous mechanism was designed to avoid the double interaction of message-based systems by providing a procedure call interface[48]. Unfortunately, the expressive powers of the supporting mechanisms are not sufficient to handle all cases of condition synchronisation. In the resource allocation example this forces a double interaction between the manager and the requesting tasks. This interaction is susceptible to race conditions and deadlock when the requesting tasks fail.

REFERENCES

1. M. Accetta, G. Robertson, M. Satyanarayanan, and M. Thompson, "The Design of a Network-Based Central File System", Department of Computer Science, Carnegie-Mellon University (August 1980).

2. P. A. Alsberg and J. D. Day, "A Principle for Resilient Sharing of Distributed Resources", *Proceedings of the Second International Conference on Software Engineering*, pp.562-570 (October 1976).

3. G. R. Andrews and F. Schneider, "Concepts and Notations for Concurrent Programming", *ACM Computing Surveys* Vol. 15(1), pp.3-44 (March 1983).

4. R. M. Balzer, "PORTS - A Method for Dynamic Interprogram communication and Job Control", *Proc. IFIPS*, pp.485-489, Atlantic City (May 1971).

5. A. B. Barak and A. Shapip, "UNIX with Satellite Processors", *Software Practice and Experience* Vol. 10, pp.383-392 (1980).

6. J. G. P. Barnes, *Programming in Ada*, Addison-Wesley (1982).

7. F. Baskett, J. Howard, and J. Montague, "Task Communication in DEMOS", *Proceedings of the Sixth ACM Symposium on Operating Systems Principles*, pp.23-32 (November 1977).

8. K. Bennett et al., "The Keele Distributed Filestore", Computer Science Report DCP/WD/80, University of Keele (August 1983).

9. G. S. Blair and D. Shepherd, "A Performance Comparison of the Ethernet and the Cambridge Digital Communication Ring", _Computer Networks_ Vol. 6(2), pp.105-115 (May 1982).

10. T. Bloom, "Evaluating Synchronisation Mechanisms", _Proceedings of the Seventh ACM Symposium on Operating System Principles_, pp.24-32, Pacific Grove (December 1979).

11. D. R. Boggs, J. F. Shoch, E. A. Taft, and R. M. Metcalfe, "Pup: An Internetwork Architecture", _IEEE Transactions on Communications_ Vol. **com-28**(4), pp.612-623 (April 1980).

12. J. van den Bos, "Comments on Ada Process Communication", _SIGPLAN Notices_ Vol. **15**(6), pp.77-81 (June 1980).

13. S.R. Bourne, "The UNIX Shell", _Bell Sys. Tech. J._ Vol. **57**(6), pp.1971-1990 (July/August 1978).

14. P. Brinch-Hansen, "Distributed Processes: A Concurrent Programming Concept", _CACM_ Vol. **21**(11), pp.934-941 (November 1978).

15. D. Brownbridge, L. Marshall, and B. Randell, "The Newcastle Connection", _Software Practice and Experience_ Vol. **12**(12), pp.1147-1162 (December 1982).

16. L. M. Casey and N. Shelness, "A Domain Structure for Distributed Computer Systems", _Proceedings of the Sixth ACM Symposium on Operating System Principles_ (November 1977).

17. D. Cheriton, M. A. Malcolm, L. S. Melen, and G. R. Sager, "Thoth, a Portable Real-time Operating System", _CACM_ Vol. **22**(2), pp.105-115 (1979).

References

18. D. Cheriton and W. Zwaenepoel, "The Distributed V Kernel and its Performance for Diskless Workstations", *Proceedings of the Ninth ACM Symposium on Operating System Principles*, pp.128-139, Bretton Wood, New Hampshire (October 1983).

19. W. Croft et al., "A Unix-Based Local Network with Load Balancing", *Computer*, pp.55-66 (April 1982).

20. R. B. Dannenberg, "Resource Sharing in a Network of Personal Computers", CMU-CD-82-152, Department of Computer Science, Carnegie-Mellon University (December 1982).

21. D. W. Davies and R. W. Watson, "Hierarchy", pp. 94-138 in *Distributed Systems - Architecture and Implementation*, ed. B. W. Lampson, Springer-Verlag (1981).

22. U.S. Department of Defense, "Requirements for Ada Programming Support Environment - Stoneman", DOD (February 1980).

23. U.S. Department of Defense, "Reference Manual for the Ada Programming Language", ANSI/MIL-STD 1815 A, (January 1983).

24. Department of Computer Science, Carnegie-Mellon University, "Research in Personal Computing at Carnegie-Mellon University", (October 1980).

25. J. Dion, "The Cambridge File Server", *ACM, Operating Systems Review* Vol. 14(4), pp.26-35 (October 1980).

26. V. A. Downes and S. J. Goldsack, "The use of the Ada Language for Programming a Distributed System", *The Real Time Programming Workshop*, Graz (April 1980).

27. P. Enslow and T. Saponas, "Distributed and Decentralised Control in Fully Distributed Processing Systems - A Survey of Applicable Models", GIT-ICS-81/02, Georgia Institute of Technology (February 1981).

28. P. H. Enslow, "What is a 'Distributed' Processing System?", *Computer* Vol. 11(1), pp.13-21 (January 1978).

29. W. Eventoff, D. Harvey, and R. Price, "The Rendezvous and Monitor Concept: Is there an Efficience Difference?", *Proceedings of the ACM-SIGPLAN Symposium on the Ada Programming Language*, SIGPLAN 15,11, pp.156-165, Boston (November 1980).

30. J. A. Feldman, "High Level Programming for Distributed Computing", CACM Vol. 22(1), pp.353-68 (June 1979).

31. C. H. Forsyth, "Support for Tasking in the Run-Time System", Ada Workbench Compiler Project 1981, Appendix G. YCS.48, University of York (1982).

32. W. M. Gentleman, "Message Passing Between Sequential Processes: the Reply Primitive and the Administrator Concept", *Software Practice and Experience* Vol. 11(5), pp.435-466 (May 1981).

33. D. K. Gifford, "Weighted Voting for Replicated Data", *Proceedings of the Seventh ACM Symposium on Operating Systems Principles*, pp.150-162 (December 1979).

34. D. K. Gifford, "Cryptographic Sealing for Information Secrecy and Authentication", CACM Vol. 25(4), pp.274-286 (April 1982).

35. C. Gram and F.R. Hertweck, "Command Languages: Design Considerations and Basic Concepts", pp. 43-67 in *Command Languages*, ed. C. Unger, North-Holland Publishing Co. (1975).

36. File Transfer Protocol Implementors Group, *A Network Independent File Transfer Protocol*, National Physical Laboratory, Teddington (February 1981).

37. A. N. Habermann and I. Nassi, "Efficient Implementation of Ada Tasks", CMU-CS-80-103, Department of Computer Science, Carnegie-Mellon University (January 1980).

38. S. Haridi, J. Bauner, and G. Svensson, "An Implementation and Empirical Evaluation of the Tasking Facilities in Ada - Summary", *SIGPLAN Notices* Vol. 16(2), pp.35-47 (February 1981).

References

39. A. Herbert, "The User Interface to the Cambridge Model Distributed System", *Second International Conference on Distributed Systems*, Versailles (6-10 April 1980).

40. P. Hilfinger, "Implementation Strategies for Ada Tasking Idioms", *Proceedings of the AdaTEC Conference on Ada*, pp.26-30, Arlington (October 1982).

41. C. A. R. Hoare, "Communicating Sequential Processes", *CACM* Vol. 21(8), pp.666-677 (August 1978).

42. E. Holler, "The National Software Works (NSW)", pp. 421-442 in *Distributed Systems - Architecture and Implementation*, ed. B. W. Lampson, Springer-Verlag (1981).

43. E. Holler, "Multiple Copy Update", pp. 284-308 in *Distributed Systems - Architecture and Implementation*, ed. B. W. Lampson, Springer-Verlag (1981).

44. R. C. Holt, "An Overview of TUNIS: A UNIX Look-Alike Written in Concurrent Euclid", TR CSRG-140, Computer Systems Research Group, University of Toronto (April 1982).

45. R. C. Holt, "A Short Introduction to Concurrent Euclid", *SIGPLAN Notices* Vol. 17(5), pp.60-80 (May 1982).

46. F. Hopgood, "Practical Aspects of Current Distributed Computer Research", *Online Mini-Computer Forum* (November 1978).

47. T. Horsley and W. Lynch, "Pilot: A Software Engineering Case Study", *Proceedings of the 4th International Conference on Software Engineering*, pp.94-98, IEEE (1979).

48. J. D. Ichbiah et al., "Rationale For The Design Of The Green Programming Language", Honeywell, Inc. and Cii Honeywell Bull (March 1979).

49. J. D. Ichbiah et al., "Reference Manual For The Green Programming Language", Honeywell, Inc. and Cii Honeywell Bull (March 1979).

50. J. Israel, J. G. Mitchell, and H. Sturgis, "Separating Data from Function in a Distributed File System", pp. 17-27 in *Operating Systems: Theory and Practice*, ed. D. Lanciaux, North-Holland Publishing Company (1979).

51. E. D. Jensen, "The Honeywell Experimental Distributed Processor - An Overview", *Computer* Vol. 11(1) (January 1978).

52. W. H. Jessop, "Ada and Distributed Systems", Technical Report #81-01-06, Department of Computer Science, University of Washington Seattle (January 1981).

53. W. H. Jessop, "Ada Packages and Distributed Systems", *SIGPLAN Notices* Vol. 17(2), pp.28-36 (February 1982).

54. M. A. Johnson, "Ring Byte Stream protocol Specification", Computing Laboratory, University of Cambridge (April 1980).

55. A. Jones and A. Ardo, "Comparative Efficiency of Different Implementations of the Ada Rendezvous", *Proceedings of the AdaTEC Conference on Ada*, pp.212-223, Arlington (October 1982).

56. A. K. Jones et al., "StarOS, a Multiprocessor Operating System for the Support of Task Forces", *Proceedings of the Seventh ACM Symposium on Operating System Principles*, pp.117-127, Pacific Grove, California (December 1979).

57. A. Karshmer, D. DePree, and J. Phelan, "The New Mexico State University Ring-Star System: A Distributed UNIX Environment", *Software Practice and Experience* Vol. 13(12), pp.1157-1168 (December 1983).

58. B. Kernighan and J. Mashey, "The UNIX Programming Environment", *Software Practice and Experience* Vol. **9**, pp.1-15 (1979).

59. B. W Kernighan and D. M. Ritchie, *The C Programming Language*, Prentice-Hall Inc., New Jersey (1978).

60. B. W. Kernighan and P.J. Plauger, *Software Tools in Pascal*, Addison-Wesley Publishing Co., Reading,MA (1981).

References

61. B. W. Kernighan and R. Pike, *The UNIX Programming Environment*, Prentice-Hall (1984).

62. L. Lamport, "Time, Clocks, and the Ordering of Events in a Distributed System", *CACM* Vol. 21(7), pp.558-565 (July 1978).

63. B. Lampson and D. Redell, "Experience with Processes and Monitors in Mesa", *CACM* Vol. 23(2), pp.105-117 (February 1980).

64. B. W. Lampson, "Atomic Transactions", pp. 246-264 in *Distributed Systems - Architecture and Implementation*, ed. B. W. Lampson, Springer-Verlag (1981).

65. A. Langsford, "What are the Justifications for Distributed Processing", AERE-R 8376, Computer Science and Systems Division, AERE Harwell (April 1976).

66. G. Le Lann, "Motivations, Objectives and Characterization of Distributed Systems", pp. 1-9 in *Distributed Systems - Architecture and Implementation, An Advanced Course, Lecture Notes in Computer Science 105*, ed. B. Lampson, Springer-Verlag (1981).

67. G. Le Lann, "Error Recovery", pp. 371-376 in *Distributed Systems - Architecture and Implementation, An Advanced Course, Lecture Notes in Computer Science 105*, ed. B. Lampson, Springer-Verlag (1981).

68. H. Lauer and E. Satterwaite, "The Impact of Mesa on System Design", *Proceedings of the 4th International Conference on Software Engineering*, pp.174-182, IEEE (1979).

69. H. Ledgard, J. A. Whiteside, A. Singer, and W. Seymour, "The Natural Language of Interactive Systems", *Communications of the ACM* Vol. 23(10), pp.556-563 (October 1980).

70. B. Liskov et al., "CLU Reference Manual", MIT/LCS/TR-225, Laboratory for Computer Science, M.I.T. (October 1979).

71. B. Liskov, "Primitives for Distributed Computing", Proceedings of the Seventh ACM Symposium on Operating System Principals, pp.33-43, Pacific Grove, California (December 1979).

72. B. Liskov, "On Linguistic Support for Distributed Programs", IEEE Transactions on Software Engineering Vol. SE-8(3), pp.203-210 (May 1982).

73. B. Liskov and R. Scheifler, "Guardians and Actions: Linguistic Support for Robust, Distributed Programs", ACM Transactions on Programming Languages and Systems Vol. 5(3), pp.381-404 (July 1983).

74. B. Liskov and M. Herlihy, "Issues in Process and Communication Structure for Distributed Programs", Proceedings Third Symposium on Reliability in Distributed Software and Database Systems, pp.123-132, Florida (October 1983).

75. H. Lycklama and C. Christensen, "UNIX Time-Sharing System: A Minicomputer Satellite Processor System", Bell Sys. Tech. J. Vol. 57(6), pp.2103-2113 (1978).

76. R. Metcalfe and D. Boggs, "Ethernet: Distributed Packet Switching For Local Computer Networks", CACM Vol. 19(7), pp.395-404 (July 1976).

77. J. G. Mitchell, W. Maybury, and R. Sweet, "Mesa Language Manual Verson 5.0", CSL-79-3, Palo Alto Research Center, Xerox (April 1979).

78. J. G. Mitchell and J. Dion, "A Comparison of Two Network-Based File Servers", CACM Vol. 25(4), pp.233-245 (April 1982).

79. J. Murdie, "Functional Specification of the York Ada Workbench Compiler, Release 1", YCS.62, Department of Computer Science, University of York (December 1983).

80. R. Needham, "System Aspects of the Cambridge Ring", Proceedings of the Seventh ACM Symposium on Operating System Principles, pp.82-86, Pacific Grove, California (December 1979).

81. R. M. Needham and A. J. Herbert, The Cambridge Distributed Computing System, Addison-Wesley Publishing Company, London (1982).

82. D. A. Nowitz and M. E. Lesk, "Implementation of a Dial-Up Network of UNIX Systems", Proceedings of the COMPCON 80 Fall Distributed Computing Conference, pp.483-486, Washington DC (September 1980).

83. D. Parker et al., "Detection of Mutual Inconsistency in Distributed Systems", IEEE Transaction on Software Engineering Vol. **SE-9**(3), pp.240-247 (May 1983).

84. G. Popek, B. Walker, et al., "LOCUS A Network Transparent, High Reliability Distributed System", Proceedings of the Eighth ACM Symposium on Operating Systems Principles, pp.169-177, Pacific Grove, California (December 1981).

85. I. C. Pyle and I. C. Wand, "Ada Compiler Project", SRC Grant GR/B 06987, Department of Computer Science, University of York (1979).

86. I. C. Pyle, The Ada Programming Language, Prentice Hall International (1981).

87. B. Randell, P. A. Lee, and P. C. Treleaven, "Reliability Issues, in Computing System Design", ACM Computing Surveys Vol. 10(2), pp.123-165 (June 1978).

88. R. F. Rashid, "An Inter-Process Communication Facility for UNIX", CMU-CS-80-124, Department of Computer Science, Carnegie-Mellon University (March 1980).

89. R. F. Rashid and G. G. Robertson, "Accent: A communication oriented network operating system kernel", Proceedings of the Eighth ACM Symposium on Operating Systems Principles, pp.64-75, Pacific Grove, California (December 1981).

90. D. Redell et al., "Pilot: An Operating System for a Personal Computer", CACM Vol. 23(2), pp.81-92 (February 1980).

91. P. F. Reynolds, J. Knight, and J. Urguhart, "The Implementation and Use of Ada on a Distributed System with High Reliability Requirements", Final Report on NASA Grant Number: NAG-1-260, Department of Applied Mathematics and Computer Science, University of Virginia (March 1983).

92. D. M. Ritchie and K. Thompson, "The UNIX Time-Sharing System", Bell Sys. Tech. J. Vol. 57(6), pp.1905-1929 (1978).

93. L. Rowe and K. Birman, "A Local Network Based on the UNIX Operating System", IEEE Transactions on Software Engineering Vol. SE-8(2), pp.137-146 (March 1982).

94. M. Satyanarayanan, M. Accetta, G. Robertson, and M. Thompson, "Synergistic File Systems for a Local Network", Department of Computer Science, Carnegie-Mellon University (August 1980).

95. A. Silberschatz, "On the Synchronisation Mechanism of the Ada Language", SIGPLAN Notices Vol. 16(2), pp.96-103 (February 1981).

96. M. H. Solomon and R. A. Finkel, "The Roscoe Distributed Operating System", Proceedings of the Seventh ACM Symposium on Operating Systems Principles, pp.108-114 (December 1979).

97. R. Stammers et al., "A Feasibility Study to Determine the Applicability of Ada and APSE in a Multi-Microprocessor Distributed Environment", SPL International, Research Centre, The Charter, Abingdon, OX14 3LZ, UK (March 1983).

98. J. Stroet, "An Alternative to the Communication Primitives in Ada", SIGPLAN Notices Vol. 15(12), pp.62-74 (December 1980 tasking).

99. A. S. Tanenbaum, "A Distributed Interactive Computer System", Rapport IR-20, Vrije Universiteit, Amsterdam (June 1977).

References

100. R. H. Thomas, "A Majority Consensus Approach to Concurrency Control for Multiple Copy Databases", *ACM Transactions on Database Systems* Vol. 4(2), pp.180-209 (June 1979).

101. K. Thompson, "UNIX Time-Sharing System: UNIX Implementation", *Bell Sys. Tech. J.* Vol. 57(6), pp.1931-1946 (1978).

102. M. Thompson, G. Robertson, M. Satyanarayanan, and M. Accetta, *Spice File System*, Department of Computer Science, Carnegie-Mellon University (September 1980).

103. B. Walker et al., "The LOCUS Distributed Operating System", *Proceedings of the Ninth ACM Symposium on Operating System Principles*, pp.49-70, Bretton Woods, New Hampshire (October 1983).

104. I. C. Wand and J. Holden, "Towards a Run-Time System for Ada", YCS.29, Department of Computer Science, University of York (1979).

105. P. Wegner and S. Smolka, "Processes, Tasks, and Monitors: A Comparative Study of Concurrent Programming Primitives", *IEEE Transaction on Software Engineering* Vol. SE-9(4), pp.446-462 (July 1983).

106. A. J. Wellings, "Distributed Operating Systems and the Ada Programming Language", D. Phil. Thesis, Department of Computer Science, University of York (April 1984).

107. A. J. Wellings, D. Keeffe, and G. M. Tomlinson, "A Problem with Ada and Resource Allocation", *Ada Letters* Vol. 3(4) (January, February 1984).

108. J. Welsh and A. M. Lister, "A Comparative Study of Task Communication in Ada", *Software Practice and Experience* Vol. 11(3), pp.257-290 (March 1981).

109. M. V. Wilkes and D. J. Wheeler, "The Cambridge Digital Communication Ring", *Local Area Communication Networks Symposium*, Mitre Corp. and National Bureau of Standards, Boston (May 1979).

110. M. V. Wilkes and R. M. Needham, "The Cambridge Model Distributed System", ACM, Operating Systems Review Vol. **13**(5) (1980).

111. N. Wirth, Programming in Modula-2, Second Edition, Springer-Verlag (1983).

112. A. Wupit, "Comparison of UNIX Network Systems", 1983 ACM Conference on Personal and Small Computers, pp. 99-108, San Diego, California (December 1983).

113. Xerox, "ALTO: A Personal Computer System", Hardware Manual", Technical Report, Xerox Palo Alto Research Centre (May 1979).

114. S. J. Young, Real Time Languages: Design and Development, Ellis Horwood Publishers, Chichester (1982).

Index

A

Abort, 23, 98
Absolute pathname, 31
Accent, 9, 14, 16
Accept, 63, 195
Access control permissions, 103
Active i-node table, 116
Active task, 194, 203
  distributed systems, 10
Ada language, 6, 10, 13, 105, 193
  ANSI standard, 193
  constraints, 105
  reference manual, 10, 195
  run-time support, 47
Ada packages, 201
Ada tasking, 7, 10, 13, 15, 16, 18, 19, 46, 57, 61, 93, 101, 107, 114, 125, 193
  abort, 62, 197, 198, 210, 212, 218
  attribute, 199
  attribute 'callable', 199
  attribute 'count', 199, 204, 207, 215
  attribute 'terminate', 199
  creation, 73, 90, 105
  dynamic creation, 61, 198, 222
  evaluation of rendezvous, 199
  interrupt entries, 24
  model, 193
  optimisation, 115
  rendezvous times, 127
  restrictions in file server, 105
  scheduling, 92
  scope rules, 222
  storage overhead, 105
  support, 83, 87, 90
  synchronisation overhead, 107
  task access variables, 197
  task types, 197
  termination, 62, 73, 105
Adjoining naming domains, 11
Alto, 9
Arachne, 12, 16
Argument, 51
  passing, 52, 64, 69
Asymmetric naming scheme, 194
Atomic transaction, 23, 38

B

Basic block, 85, 96
  port, 85
  protocol, 85, 129
Bloom's methodology, 193, 201
Blue Book protocols, 11
Broadcast, 36
Buffer allocation, 114
Buffer representation, 113
Busy wait, 133, 212

C

C, 6, 83, 105, 125
Cambridge Distributed System, 9
Cambridge File Server, 41, 129
Cambridge Ring, 22, 83, 129, 131
  interface, 85
  minipackets, 85
Client, 10, 16, 102, 120
Clone, 49, 58, 103
CLU, 7
Cocanet, 11, 30
Command interpreter, 39
Command language, 50
Command line analysis, 53
Communication and synchronisation, 194
Communication failure, 22, 97
Communication overheads, 129
Concurrent Euclid, 14
Condition synchronisation, 200, 203
Controller task, 108, 110, 120
Crash, 121, 123
CSP, 16, 194

D

Data transaction performance figures, 130
Deadlock, 210, 212, 218
Device drivers, 85
Direct naming scheme, 16
Directory, 31, 35, 112, 123
Disk buffer cache, 112, 113, 119

Index

Disk volume 36, 112, 115
  identifier, 115, 121
  layout, 115
  mounting, 116
Distributed computing, 2
  motives, 2
Distributed name server, 40
Distributed operating system, 10, 11
Distribution and replication, 104
DP, 194
Dup, 44
Duplicate copy, 124
Duplicate file, 32, 38, 40
  creation, 35, 117
  deletion, 35, 117
  synchronisation, 37, 117
Duplicate i-node, 34
Duplicate mode, 34
Duplicate volume, 34, 115
Dynamic storage allocation, 106

E

Ease of use, 199, 200
Entry, 195
  family, 114, 198, 207
  interrupt, 24
Entry call, 16, 21, 23
  conditional, 21, 62, 128
  timed, 21, 24, 128
Ethernet, 129, 131
Exception, 22, 23, 92, 95, 98
  handling, 7, 10, 87, 92
  no_reader, 24, 64, 99
  no_writer, 24, 99
  tasking_error, 198
Exec, 45, 49, 54, 57
Exit, 45
Expressive power, 199, 200, 203

F

File control, 44, 48
File copies, 34
File creation, 39
File deletion, 39
File location, 36
File protection, 31, 38
File replication, 30, 31, 32, 37, 38, 124
  control, 40
File selection control, 39
File server, 68, 101
  communication protocol, 41, 121
  implementation constraints, 105
  kernel traps, 137
  limits to parallelism, 114
  operation times, 137
  operations, 48
  private interface, 101, 119, 120
  public interface, 101
  request Medium, 48, 102, 103, 109
  structure, 107
File server request Medium, 98
  performance evaluation, 134
  low-level naming scheme, 33
  object naming, 33
File system context, 48
Fork, 13, 45, 46, 49, 54, 57

G

Garbage collection, 61, 222
Generics, 7
Global port, 96
Green language, 193, 197, 201
  Rationale, 194, 206
Guarded, 195

H

Hierarchical file store, 8, 29, 101, 113

I

I-list, 115
I-map, 35, 38, 115
I-node, 34, 35, 38, 111, 115, 116, 117, 120, 122
  remote activity, 118
  table manager, 117
I-number, 34
  allocation, 35
  global, 34, 35, 101, 112, 115
  local, 115
I-sequence number, 34
Indirect blocks, 116
Indirect naming scheme, 16, 194
  remote active, 121
Integrated distributed file system, 29, 42
Inter-process communication, 40
Inter-program communication, 10, 15, 46, 47, 83, 93, 101, 107, 129
  protocol, 22
Interrupts, 23, 85, 132

K

Keele distributed file store, 30

L

Lifeline, 58, 98, 104
Link, 16, 36, 110, 194
Load balancing, 9, 143
Local area network, 29
Local disk storage, 29

Index

Local duplicate, 39, 136
Local master, 39, 136
Locking, 117, 122
LOCUS, 12, 30, 33, 37, 42
Logical device interface, 99
Logical file, 33
Logical file, I/O, 119
LSI-11/23, 83, 85, 101, 131

M

Manager task, 108, 116, 117
Master copy, 38
Master file, 32, 33, 38, 40
Master volumes, 34
Medium, 16, 17, 23, 41, 69, 93
   allocation, 93, 128
   broadcast, 47, 121
   capability, 17
   deallocation, 93, 128
   error handling, 95
   file server request, 48, 98, 102, 103, 109
   global, 47, 120
   implementation, 93
   lifeline, 58, 98, 104
   open file, 102, 110, 148
   reader, 17
   reliable, 41
   remote i-node, 118, 120
   reply, 95, 102
   reply capability, 93
   transfer, 95
   transfer capability, 93
   unreliable, 121
   writer, 16
Mesa, 7, 9, 10, 15
Message structure, 94
Message type, 94
Message-based communication, 16
Methods of distribution, 9
Modularity, 199, 201
Monitor, 199
Mount table, 37
Multiple copy, 32
Multiple copy update problem, 33
Mutual exclusion, 200, 203
My reference, 122

N

Nassi-Habermann optimisation, 115, 140
National Software Works, 11
Network partition, 32, 99
Network server, 96, 133
Network transparency, 29, 30, 31
Newcastle Connection, 11, 30
NMSU Ring-Star System, 9, 12

No-wait send, 18, 21
Non-sharable programs, 99
Nowait, 49, 61

O

Open file, 110
   Medium, 102, 110, 148
   table, 111
Operating context, 44
Overlay times, 128
Overlays, 106

P

Package, 69
Parameter passing, 69
Parasitic users, 39
Passive task, 194, 203
Pathname, 31, 35, 73, 101, 113, 124
Pathname search, 38, 124, 144
Per task user area, 87
Performance evaluation, 127
Performance transparency, 142
Personal computer, 32, 42
Physical I/O, 108, 114
Pilot, 9, 15
Pipe, 55
Pipeline, 61
Pipes, 51
Port, 16, 194
Primary context, 49
Primary copy, 32
Private interface, 41
Process naming, 16
Process synchronisation, 17
Program execution, 47, 79, 103
Program expansion, 90
Program invocation, 48
   background, 51, 52, 57, 61
   conditional, 53, 57, 61
   foreground, 57
Program loading, 97, 115
Program overlaying, 90
Program swapping, 90
Programming support environment, 10
PULSE command interface, 51
PULSE distributed file system, 27, 29, 101
   performance evaluation, 134
PULSE expression of shell commands, 57
PULSE kernel, 10, 46, 83
   current status, 99
   performance evaluation, 127
   tasking limitations, 93
   uniform access to, 15
   file system, 29
   IPC, 15
   user interface, 43

PULSE shell, 39
PULSE shell implementation, 61
PULSE system facilities, 46
Pup protocol, 129

R

Race condition, 216
Redirection of I/O, 61
Reliable Medium, 41
Remote duplicate, 39
   locating, 37
Remote duplicate volumes, 37
   access, 111
Remote files, 118
Remote invocation send, 19, 21
Remote master, 39, 136
Remote procedure call, 111, 120
Remote program execution, 79
Remote volumes, 36
Removable disks, 30
Rendezvous, 10, 16, 114
Rendezvous support, 90
Repeatable transaction, 23, 41
Repeatable transactions, 122
Replicated data, 32
Replication, 29
Requirements for a synchronisation
   mechanism, 199
Resource allocation problem, 211
Resource deallocation, 23, 103
Resource scheduling, 200

S

Satellite processors, 9
Secondary context, 49
Select statement, 127, 195, 203
Semaphore, 199
Server, 10, 16
Server task, 194
Set exit status, 49
Setuid, 45
Set_map, 104, 110
Shared memory, 10
Shared resource, 195, 199
Shell, 43
Shell, 51, 53
Signal, 23
Single naming domain, 12, 31, 32
Software generated interrupts, 23
Software tools, 67
Spice, 9, 14, 42
   file system, 32, 41
Stable storage, 96
Stack limit checking, 90
Stand-alone, 29, 33, 37

StarOs, 12
Sun work station, 131
Super block, 115
Synchronise on reference, 37, 39
Synchronised send, 19, 21
Syntax tree, 53

T

Task control block, 87
Thoth operating system, 20, 24
Time, 38
Timed entry call, 196
Timeout, 15, 21, 23, 24, 97, 122, 123, 132,
   197, 198
Transaction number, 122
Transferring Medium capabilities, 47
Tunis, 14
Type secure communication, 22, 27

U

UNIX, 4, 8, 9, 11, 13, 23, 31, 33, 38, 40,
   43, 53, 68, 72, 103, 127
   block I/O, 113
   command interface, 51
   file access permissions, 6
   file system, 4
   process model, 6
   system facilities, 44
Unlink, 110
Unrelated naming domains, 11
Unreliable Medium, 121
Unsafe data, 22, 94
User programming, 67

V

V distributed kernel, 131
Variant record, 22
Version number, 34, 38
Version vectors, 32
Virtual address space, 90
Virtual circuit, 22, 97
Voting, 32

W

Wait, 45, 49, 61, 103
Worker task, 62, 73, 108, 109, 120, 123
Working directory, 31, 103, 124

X

X25, 11
XDFS, 129

Y

York Ada, 127
   compiler, 83, 90

A.P.I.C. Studies in Data Processing
General Editors: Fraser Duncan and M. J. R. Shave

1. Some Commercial Autocodes. A Comparative Study*
   E. L. Willey, A. d'Agapeyeff, Marion Tribe, B. J. Gibbens and Michelle Clarke

2. A Primer of ALGOL 60 Programming
   E. W. Dijkstra

3. Input Language for Automatic Programming*
   A. P. Yershov, G. I. Kozhukhin and U. Voloshin

4. Introduction to System Programming*
   Edited by Peter Wegner

5. ALGOL 60 Implementation. The Translation and Use of ALGOL 60 Programs on a Computer
   B. Randell and L. J. Russell

6. Dictionary for Computer Languages*
   Hans Breuer

7. The Alpha Automatic Programming System*
   Edited by A. P. Yershov

8. Structured Programming
   O.-J. Dahl, E. W. Dijkstra and C. A. R. Hoare

9. Operating Systems Techniques
   Edited by C. A. R. Hoare and R. H. Perrott

10. ALGOL 60 Compilation and Assessment
    B. A. Wichmann

11. Definition of Programming Languages by Interpreting Automata
    Alexander Ollongren

12. Principles of Program Design
    M. A. Jackson

*Out of print.

13. Studies in Operating Systems
    R. M. McKeag and R. Wilson
14. Software Engineering
    R. J. Perrott
15. Computer Architecture: A Structured Approach
    R. W. Doran
16. Logic Programming
    Edited by K. L. Clark and S.-A. Tärnlund
17. Fortran Optimization*
    Michael Metcalf
18. Multi-microprocessor Systems
    Y. Paker
19. Introduction to the Graphical Kernel System—GKS
    F. R. A. Hopgood, D. A. Duce, J. R. Gallop and D. C. Sutcliffe
20. Distributed Computing
    Edited by Fred B. Chambers, David A. Duce and Gillian P. Jones
21. Introduction to Logic Programming
    Christopher John Hogger
22. Lucid, the Dataflow Programming Language
    William W. Wadge and Edward A. Ashcroft
23. Foundations of Programming
    Jacques Arsac
24. Prolog for Programmers
    Feliks Kluźniak and Stanislaw Szpakowicz
25. Fortran Optimization, Revised Edition
    Michael Metcalf
26. PULSE: An Ada-based Distributed Operating System
    D. Keeffe, G. M. Tomlinson, I. C. Wand and A. J. Wellings